The Red Book

The Membership List of The Right Club, 1939

introduced and edited by

Robin Saikia

FOXLEY BOOKS
London MMX

Copyright © 2010 Robin Saikia
The right of Robin Saikia has been
asserted by him in accordance with the
Copyright, Design and Patents Acts, 1988

ISBN 978-1-905742-02-8

Published in 2010
By Foxley Books Limited

www.foxleybooks.com

The Red Book

The Membership List of The Right Club, 1939

In May 1939 Captain Archibald Maule Ramsay, a Conservative MP, formed an anti-Semitic secret society he called The Right Club. Many of its members were Nazi sympathisers and an inner core were politicians, peers of the realm, prominent socialites and officers in the armed forces. Ramsay recorded their names in a stout, red, leather-bound ledger that was seized by Special Branch in May 1940. It came to be known as The Red Book and its contents are published here in full for the first time.

Robin Saikia was educated at Winchester College and Merton College, Oxford. He is the author of *Blue Guide Hay-on-Wye*, a cultural and historical exploration of the Anglo-Welsh border town famed for its bookdealers and as the venue of the annual Guardian Hay Festival of Literature and the Arts. His latest book, *The Venice Lido*, is published by Blue Guides this summer. Forthcoming titles for Foxley Books include *Hitler's Venice* and *Hitler's London*.

Front and back cover photographs by Joachim von Halasz: The Red Book, by kind permission of the Wiener Library.

Foxley Books

Foxley Books is an independent imprint founded by the German publisher Joachim von Halasz. It is based in London and Munich and publishes primary source material to facilitate the study of history and propaganda. Reprints of key works are accompanied by introductory essays and translations.

This year sees the launch by Foxley Books of its World Propaganda Classics series. Titles will include rare classics from ancient Persia, Greece and Rome, the French and Russian Revolutions, the World Wars, the Spanish Civil War, Third Reich Germany and the Cold War.

Foxley Books is committed to publishing important texts that have had a formative influence for better or for worse on world affairs. We always welcome suggestions, ideas and submissions.

Recently published titles include:

Degenerate Art Exhibition Guide (1937)
The first bilingual edition of this Nazi classic.

The Truffle Eater (1933)
The first anti-Hitler cartoon book.

View these and other titles at:

www.foxleybooks.com

Contents

Foreword by Julia Camoys Stonor	*1*
Prologue	*3*
Introduction	*10*
The Red Book	*59*
The Right Club A-Z	*97*
Appendix 1 Particulars of Captain Ramsay's Internment under Defence Regulation 18b	*133*
Appendix 2 The Statutes of Jewry, 1275	*141*
Appendix 3 Despatch of Herbert von Dirksen to Berlin, 1939.	*144*
Selected Bibliography and Sources	*148*
Acknowledgements	*150*

Foreword

by Julia Camoys Stonor

I am Captain Archibald Maule Ramsay's cousin, the eldest daughter of Sherman Stonor, 6th Baron Camoys, and Jeanne Stourton.

My mother Jeanne was one of the great society beauties of the Thirties. She gathered around her a number of right wing admirers, known to me as 'uncles' if they were close friends or, if they came to shoot, simply as 'guns'. This book brings back many memories of my childhood at Assendon Lodge and Stonor Park during and after the war, where many of the protagonists were regular visitors, all of them part of my mother's profoundly pro-Nazi entourage and many of them blatantly active in France, Spain, Germany and England. The revealing passages about the *Anglo-German Review* recall Joachim von Ribbentrop, Hitler's ambassador in London, who part-funded the magazine and was one of my mother's lovers.

My cousin Archibald Maule Ramsay was a somewhat distant, forbidding figure, a man of volatile temper and poisonous extremes. He attracted companions of similar temperament who came to Assendon and Stonor, among them the formidable Mary Allen of the Women's Police Service, not herself a member of the Right Club, but a force to be reckoned with, consorting with Franco, Mussolini, Hitler, Goering and the Irish fascist leader Eoin O'Duffy. She became a considerable source of embarrassment to the Home Office, since the Women's Police Service was not a part of the real police but was a right wing organisation set up by Margaret Damer Dawson and Mary Allen herself, attracting many decidedly determined and somewhat 'masculine' ladies, many of them former suffragettes.

Nor can I forget one of the prominent lady members of The Right Club, Edith Cazenove, largely because our paths crossed later in life, long after the war had ended and former right wingers had happily continued to reinvent themselves. Edith was to become one of my first paying guests when I started taking lodgers in the Seventies. A sleek, plump woman, heavily bejeweled, elegant, angry and hostile, Edith could never bring herself to admit that she had been a close friend of my mother Jeanne and that she had unashamedly cultivated the most extreme right wing affiliations. Edith, along with many other Right Club members, would have been disgusted by the embarrassing fact that I had two Jewish relatives by marriage, the Slomnicka sisters, who perished, murdered in the Warsaw ghetto. They were the aunts of my late husband, Donald Robin Slomnicki Saunders, to whom I was married in 1963.

We now live in a different age, seventy years after the last entries were recorded in The Red Book, prior to the internment of many of its members under Defence Regulation 18b. Some of the episodes and characters described in these pages may at first sight seem bizarre, almost unbelievable. But they remain very real – and extremism of the sort experienced then is very much alive and kicking today. As Robin courageously suggests, perhaps the message of this book is that we should all be wary of extremist political views, however seductive they may seem to many of us personally – and however much they may seem, on the face of it, to present an easy remedy for the ills of the world.

Julia Camoys Stonor
London, June 2010

Julia Camoys Stonor is best known for her biography of her mother Jeanne, *Sherman's Wife - A wartime childhood amongst the English Catholic Aristocracy* (Desert Hearts, 2006). Her own memoirs, *Sherman's Daughter*, are to be published this October by Foxley Books.

Prologue

Tommy asked incredulously:
'And there really are these – these swine?'
'Everywhere. As I told you. In our service. In the fighting forces. On Parliamentary benches. High up in the Ministries. We've got to comb them out – we've got to! And we must do it quickly. It can't be done from the bottom – the small fry, the people who speak in the parks, who sell their wretched little news-sheets, they don't know who the big bugs are. It's the big bugs we want, they're the people who can do untold damage – and will do unless we're in time.'

Agatha Christie, *N or M?* (1941)

[Nesta Webster] is one of those people who have got one cause on the brain. It is the good old 'Jewish revolutionary' bogey. But there is a type of unstable mind which cannot rest without morbid imaginings, and the conception of a single cause simplifies thought. With this good woman it is the Jews, with some people it is the Jesuits, with others Freemasons and so on. The world is more complex than that.

Hilaire Belloc

The quiet *savoir-faire* of the British authorities in the face of crisis is always illuminating. There came a defining moment in the heavily over-mythologised 'Battle of Cable Street' when Sir Philip Game, the Commissioner of the Metropolitan Police, approached Oswald Mosley with the following schoolmasterly rebuke: 'As you can see for yourself, if you fellows go ahead from here there will be a shambles. I am not going to have that. You must call it off.' Mosley replied, rather petulantly, 'Is that an order?' On hearing that it was, he disbanded his men, and that was that. This vignette, recalling not so much the playing-fields of Eton as those of Winchester, says much about the English temperament on which Hitler and others would have done well to reflect. The green and pleasant land of free speech and civil liberty may comfortably sustain without pogrom or persecution the antics of the Mosleys, A. K. Chestertons, Archibald Ramsays, Arnold Leeses and Enoch Powells. What it will not under any circumstances tolerate is a *shambles*, which was what it very nearly got as a result of the pre-war activities of Captain Archibald Henry Maule Ramsay, Conservative MP for Peebles and South Midlothian.

Ramsay was elected to Parliament in 1931. 'Jock', as his friends knew him, went to Eton and Sandhurst and had served with the Coldstream Guards in World War I. His war record was impeccable, his early political career unexceptional. A well-connected Scottish aristocrat related to the Earls of Dalhousie, at first he did nothing more in parliament than raise a predictable clutch of routine matters, mainly touching on land and agriculture. His most distinguished appointment was as parliamentary representative on the Potato Marketing Board. By 1937, however, his public persona had changed. He aired right-wing views in the House of Commons and elsewhere, speaking of the Spanish Civil War as a crusade against communism and atheism. He became convinced that 'the Russian and Spanish revolutions, and the subversive societies in Britain' were part and parcel of a plan for world domination, 'secretly operated and controlled by World Jewry, exactly on the lines laid down in the Protocols of the Elders of Zion'. In 1938 he joined the Council of the right-wing Nordic League, contributed to the *Anglo-German Review* and was closely associated with Admiral Sir Barry Domvile, head of a leading pro-German organisation, The Link. Finally, in May 1939, he formed a secret society he called the Right Club, whose members he recorded in a stout, red leather-bound ledger that came to be known as the Red Book and that is published here in full for the first time. 'The main object of the Right Club' he said 'was to oppose and expose the activities of

Organized Jewry'. His 'first objective was to clear the Conservative Party of Jewish influence', an aim he felt certain he could achieve by 'co-ordinating the work of all the patriotic societies'. A no less important aim, shared by many of the 'patriotic societies' he sought to unify, was to avoid at all costs another European war. Right Club members were mainly of the British upper and middle class, though there were several mavericks and a cluster of hangers-on. The true blues were represented by peers and MPs like Lord Redesdale, Lord Galloway, the Duke of Wellington, Sir Peter Agnew and Sir James Edmondson, the mavericks by live-wires like William Joyce (Lord Haw-Haw), A. K. Chesterton, Arnold Spencer Leese and, as we shall see, Anna Wolkoff.

On the outbreak of World War II, the Right Club officially disbanded, but during the months of comparative inactivity now known as the ' Phoney War', Ramsay and an inner core of Right Club members held secret meetings with Barry Domvile, Oswald Mosley and others. Their objective now was to achieve a negotiated peace[1] by making more widely known their view that Britons had been misled into fighting a 'Jews' war'. Ramsay actively distributed subversive leaflets and posters extolling his anti-war, anti-Jewish line. It is also likely that he and others intended to stage a right-wing Fascist military coup, but local and international events soon to put paid to any such ambitious ideas. In any case, by May 1940 the Right Club's days were numbered, since it was by then under surveillance by MI5 and had been infiltrated by four agents under the supervision of Charles Maxwell Knight[2], head of B5b, the political subversion unit of the secret service.

---

[1] See Appendix 1, the Particulars of Ramsay's detention under Defence Regulation 18b and his detailed Replies.

[2] **Maxwell Knight, Charles Henry (1900- 1968)** MI5 officer who ran the undercover operation that led to the arrest of Tyler Kent and Anna Wolkoff and ultimately to the internment of Captain Ramsay and many other suspected Nazi sympathizers. He wrote two thrillers, *Crime Cargo* and *Gunmen's Holiday*, played the drums in a jazz band and was a Fellow of the Royal

The authorities were not at this stage overly preoccupied with Ramsay and his upper-crust right-wing friends, many of whom they had monitored assiduously throughout the Thirties. Of grave and immediate concern were the activities of the Right Club maverick Anna Wolkoff and her associate Tyler Kent, a cipher clerk at the American Embassy. Wolkoff, a volatile White Russian émigré, ran the Russian Tea Rooms, a South Kensington restaurant near Ramsay's house in Onslow Square known for good caviar and champagne and frequented by well-heeled right-wingers. Tyler Kent, according to Malcolm Muggeridge, the MI6 observer at his trial, was 'one of those intensely gentlemanly Americans who wear well-cut tailor-made suits, with waistcoat and watch-chain, drink wine instead of high-balls, and easily become furiously indignant'.

Kent, a Princeton man, saw himself as an American patriot. He was firmly against American participation in a distant and costly European war. As a cipher clerk he had seen secret documents that sharpened these feelings and made him indignant, telegrams between Roosevelt and Churchill, confirming beyond reasonable doubt that America would support France in the event of a German invasion and that she would, if necessary, join the allied cause. He made copies, intending one day to produce them as evidence of a sell-out engineered by the Roosevelt administration. Ramsay, who had been introduced to Kent by Wolkoff, saw in the presentable young American a

---

Zoological Society. He was an acknowledged expert on animals and wrote several popular books on the subject. Some of these were aimed at the generalist – *The Young Field Naturalist's Guide* (1952), *Bird Gardening* (1954), *Reptiles in Britain* (1965) – whereas others had a more specialist flavour: *How to Keep an Elephant* (1967) and *How to Keep a Gorilla* (1968). Knight was a colourful spymaster, regularly meeting his agents in seedy London hotels and disguising his own identity with a series of aliases. The cloak and dagger mystique relied to some extent on his adopting a 'maverick' persona, preferring to operate from his flat in Dolphin Square rather than from the official MI5 HQ at Thames House on Millbank. Ian Fleming was one of his agents and James Bond's chief, 'M', owes much to Knight.

trustworthy idealist who shared his anti-war views. His trust in Kent was such that he gave him the Red Book for safekeeping, feeling sure that it would be safe in Kent's South Kensington flat, hidden behind the veil of diplomatic immunity. Wolkoff, a starstruck pro-Nazi, saw how valuable the Churchill-Roosevelt documents would be to German military intelligence. She had them smuggled to Berlin via her contact at the Italian Embassy in London, the exotic naval attaché, Francesco Marigliano, Duca del Monte.

Wolkoff had no idea that her activities were being closely monitored by MI5. Lulled into a false sense of security by its *agents provocateurs*, she had written a highly incriminating letter to erstwhile Right Club member William Joyce, offering suggestions as to revised content for his now notorious 'Lord Haw-Haw' broadcasts from Radio Hamburg. MI8, meanwhile, the wireless interception unit of the secret service, had picked up radio traffic between Rome and Berlin confirming that Admiral Wilhelm Canaris of German Military Intelligence was aware of exchanges between Roosevelt and Churchill. MI5 and the Special Branch arrested Kent and Wolkoff on May 18 1940 and charged them under the Official Secrets Act. In an added complication that Ramsay could not have foreseen, the American Ambassador Joseph Kennedy, after an urgent meeting with Guy Liddell of MI5, decided to waive Kent's right to diplomatic immunity. This enabled the British to act swiftly and after the seizure of the Red Book by Special Branch its lock was forced in the Ambassador's presence, the damning list of influential names revealed.

The British Government, unsettled by a dangerous act of espionage played out on its doorstep in a secret society run by a Member of Parliament, decided to crack down on the British right wing. By the end of May 1940, in a decisive swoop masterminded by Winston Churchill, Ramsay and hundreds of others with known or suspected pro-Nazi views were arrested and detained without trial. For this draconian exercise the Government invoked the wartime security measure Defence

Regulation 18b, part of legislation designed to cover emergencies in war and deal with those suspected of collaborating with the enemy. In a meeting of the Privy Council on May 23 1940, Regulation 18b was modified by a vital addendum, Clause 1a. This small but significant refinement, somewhat like anti-terrorist measures in operation today, strengthened the Government's position considerably, increasing its powers of arrest to catch not only traitors it could verify as such but also extremists it merely suspected. Some, like Ramsay, were to remain inside for very nearly the duration of the war, their many applications for *habeas corpus* heard but for the most part dismissed. As a result, a great many Right Club members, with other prominent extremists like the Mosleys, found themselves interned without trial in Brixton, Holloway, the Isle of Man and other prisons throughout Britain. Bewildered pickpockets, burglars and bigamists found themselves rubbing shoulders with Old Etonians, high society hostesses and ramrod-straight members of the Brigade of Guards. In the peculiarly British black comedy tha ensued, some internees fared better than others. Diana Mosley wore her furs in Holloway. Mosley, finding life tough without servants, was granted the services of a couple of deferential sex offenders as valet and gofer. Ramsay was sent grouse by a well-wisher, Billy Luttman-Johnson, a Right Club member only recently released from internment himself. He memorably acknowledged this kindness with a thank-you letter written on House of Commons paper, overstamped with the mark of the Brixton censor.

From the outset there were questions in Parliament about the Right Club and the Red Book. It was an open secret that members included politicians, peers, officers in the armed forces and influential members of society. The Home Secretary, Herbert Morrison, attempted to justify the Government's refusal to publish the list. Although persistently tormented by professional gadflies like Manny Shinwell and Tom Driberg, he stonewalled them with the anodyne assertion that to publish the names would not be 'in the public interest'. It all began to look suspiciously like a cover-up. In any case, after a while, the Red Book disappeared from public view. There were stories of it attaining iconic status, of it being displayed as a totem and venerated at meetings of far-right organisations, of it possessing grail-like supernatural qualities. In reality it had come into the possession of two sisters, Right Club members, and eventually came to light in the Eighties in a solicitor's safe. It was entrusted to Professor Richard Griffiths, author of *Fellow Travellers of the Right* and *Patriotism Perverted: Captain Ramsay, the Right Club and British Anti-Semitism 1939-40*. He gave it to the Wiener Library in London where it now is, its travels at an end.

Much has been written about Right Club members, but never before has the list been published as just that – the List. There are different views on the rights and wrongs of publishing the Red Book in this way. The charitable view is that there is no virtue in raking the ashes, since the true villains on the list are sufficiently well-documented: it would be unfair and unhelpful to hold a largely misguided or blameless majority up to posthumous scrutiny: many of the Right Club were, after all, naïve and ill-informed and had no serious conception of the extreme ideology they had signed up to. The other view is that all secret societies devoted to extremism of any sort are very dangerous: they often rely on cultivating the support of the naïve and the well-meaning in order to gain the critical mass they need to move forward: open scrutiny of a secret list acts as a warning, as a living example of how wrong-headed and potentially dangerous a group of individuals can be when fate or force of will brings them together, however innocent or ill-informed many of the group may have been. Whichever view readers take, I hope that this book will help them form a clearer picture of a difficult period in history – of its inherent absurdities and contradictions as well as of its evils.

Robin Saikia
London, June 2010

Introduction

> Most of my researches in the modern period, from *The Reactionary Revolution* (1966) through *Marshal Pétain* (1970) and *Fellow Travellers of the Right* (1980), to my forthcoming book on anti-Semitism in the 1939-1940 period in Britain, have been undertaken because of a belief I hold: that most people when they wake up in the morning, look in the mirror and say to themselves 'I am all right; my attitudes and actions are justified'. And then some of these people go out and do, or get involved in, the most dreadful things. My aim, throughout, has been to try and work out such people's reasons for action, or the justifications they make to themselves. Only thereby can we learn how to deal with such people and attitudes in the future.
>
> Richard Griffiths, *Marshal Pétain*

Country Life in the Thirties was as reassuring a magazine then as it is today. Each number contained material predictable in subject, scope and treatment: a photograph of a pretty girl; how best to scare pigeons using stuffed owls; the ancestry of the Shepherd Dog; revelations from the Duc de Noailles that death duties in France were every bit as crippling as those in Britain; Sir Rowland Sperling's stark analysis of the rabbit problem. The March 1936 number, however, broke with convention when it printed an unusual spoof by one 'Ignatius Phayre', entitled 'Hitler as a Countryman – The "Squire" of Wachenfeld'. This was a 'lifestyle' piece that depicted the Führer as a reluctant celebrity with a human side, forced by cruel fame into reluctant seclusion, sustained by the humility and good humour that had seen him through his early setbacks as a painter and decorator, comforted throughout the lonely hours of siege either by his pets or by the occasional visitor.

Let me say at once that Herr Hitler has keenly artistic tastes. He paints in water-colour; he had early ambitions to become an architect. As for literature, one remembers him as the author of a colossal "best seller": I mean his political testament *Mein Kampf* (My Struggle), which sold 3,000,000 copies. It was from the royalties on this work – which is known as the "Nazi Bible" – that this shy, retiring man was enabled to extend and develop his ideal Bavarian home. What is now Haus Wachenfeld – a cosy but modest *chalet* perched at 2,000 feet above Berchtesgaden – was formerly just a peasant's cottage where Herr Hitler was cared for by his widowed sister, Frau Angela Raubel. With his gradual rise to power, that rude frame shack blossomed into a villa. Later on it was added to and ornamented by its owner. More and more land was acquired, and with it some village property. Today, quite an estate is laid out on these mountain slopes. The inner sanctum, with the *chalet* itself, is surrounded by barbed wire; and armed guards keep off well-meaning admirers and excursion visitors, who flock hither and thither from all parts of Germany.

The expansion of the Wachenfeld estate was an unmistakeable metaphor for Hitler's territorial ambitions in Europe, the chilling reference to barbed wire emphasing the point. 'Ignatius Phayre' warmed to his subject, reiterating a view held by Lady Londonderry and others, that Hitler was a kind man, as fond of dogs as he was of children.

Haus Wachenfeld is necessarily the political citadel of the head of the German Government. Here he is often abroad soon after dawn, clad in plus fours, and with his retriever Muck, or else his trained Alsatian Blonda, trotting at his heels. One or other of these will be carrying on its back a little hamper containing tomato sandwiches and fruit, with a couple of bottles of mineral water. Then amid the pines, or on some commanding knoll beside a cross and wayside shrine, Herr Hitler will sit down to ponder his problems and speeches.

With hindsight, seventy years later, it seems easy to dismiss this as being in poor taste. Yet to do so would be wrong, since 'Ignatius

Phayre', said to be the political writer William George Fitzgerald, had identified and satirised a remarkable phenomenon widely prevalent in the upper reaches of British society in the Thirties, a persistent failure to acknowledge Hitler's true nature, a failure that brought with it a tendency to try to minimize and normalize the well-publicized and very disturbing domestic and international policies of the Third Reich. The following is a genuine document, a letter to Hitler from the mistress of Right Club member Jock Houston. No spoof, it was written and sent in deadly earnest.

15, Thornton Avenue
London, SW2
31/8/39

The Führer and Reichskanzler
Adolf Hitler
Reichskanzlei
Berlin

Dear Herr Hitler,

As an Englishwoman who was very often in Germany, I wish you to know that I have unlimited trust in you.

Yours,
Mollie Hiscox

In what manner of social and political landscape could such a letter be written with a straight face? To begin with, Britain in the Thirties was a fragmented and unhappy landscape where, according to Quentin Bell, it was "hell", and "to be young and alive was bloody, thankless, a maelstrom of strife…" Whilst the Left saw hope for a welcome deliverance from social injustice in the changing post-war world, the Right saw little but a precipitate erosion of all it held dear. The working-class felt hard-done-by after the Depression and was beginning to lose faith in government and to express open resentment of its masters. The middle-class felt then, as it is beginning to feel again today, an uneasy sense that prosperity and upward mobility might be blighted by recession, war and immigration. The upper class felt a sense of responsibility, a duty to stop the rot: deeply mistrustful of the ballot box and the other paraphernalia of democracy, they were deeply entrenched in a feudal system where ties of land, kin, school and regiment conferred a sense of absolute entitlement, a belief that only a small handful of the privileged and elect were fit to act for the greater good of a nation in crisis. And glowing examples of political and cultural reversal in the face of crisis were to be seen in Europe: if Hitler and Mussolini had unified and revitalised their countries with dramatic success after the wreckage of World War I, why couldn't a leader of similar calibre do the same for Britain? At all events, there was a sinking feeling across the whole of society that much was now in jeopardy that had previously been taken for granted – traditional values, the Empire, England as the domain exclusively of Englishmen and, above all, peace. Across the board, discontent and uncertainty spawned innumerable pressure groups, movements, organizations, dining-clubs, debating societies, magazines, books, pamphlets, periodicals, publishing imprints, handbills, cadres, factions, cults, sects, open societies, secret societies, leagues, guilds, kinships. Scapegoats and public enemies were routinely identified and held up for chastisement, in particular Jews, Bolsheviks, Liberals and foreigners. It was against this turbulent background that Ramsay founded the Right Club.

The 'patriotic societies' he sought to unify differed greatly in size, agenda and efficiency. There were well-established outfits like the Anglo-German Fellowship, Mosley's British Union of Fascists, The Link, the Imperial Fascist League, the Nordic League and the January Club. Then there were more eccentric fraternities such as the White Knights of Britain, the English Mistery, the Anti-Vivisection League and the group that had no official name but is known to historians simply as the Lady Alexandra Hardinge Group. Since Ramsay himself was connected to many of these societies, he was ideally placed to recruit members from their ranks for his new enterprise. Unsurprisingly, most of them hailed from the aristocracy or the middle class. Quite a few were Members of Parliament, peers and officers in the armed forces. Others were active pro-Nazis and leading or founder members of established right-wing groups such as The Link, the Imperial Fascist League, the Nordic League and the British Union of Fascists. The remainder were drawn from the ready ranks of socialites, dowagers, hangers-on, the lonely and the eccentric. Ramsay recorded their names in the 'Red Book'. A majority of members received the Right Club's silver badge which showed an image of an eagle killing a snake accompanied by the letters 'PJ', standing for a popular anti-Semite motto of the time, 'Perish Judah!' A majority also made a financial contribution of some sort, either pledging annual subscriptions of between half-a-crown and a guinea, or making generous lump-sum donations of between £5 and £100. Despite its agenda, the Right Club remained up and running on a strictly 'informal' basis during the first months of war, Ramsay and his associates lobbying vigorously for what he called an 'honourable negotiated peace'. Privately, they remained committed to the dissemination of their old anti-Semite line, struggling to impart credibility to a new line they now had to take: that the true patriot was one who would fight for King and Country against Hitler but would nevertheless continue to do everything in his power to bring about the downfall of a still greater enemy, international Jewry.

Anyone who has attended a British public school, served in a British regiment or been sent to a British prison will immediately recognize the boyish excitement and sense of illicit conspiracy that surrounded the formation of secret societies and clubs in the Thirties. To have done time in all three is to be trebly wise. The January Club, a discussion group set up in 1934 to attract the smart set to the predominantly working-class British Union of Fascists, was a good example of one of the exclusive patriotic societies. Billy Luttman-Johnson, donor of grouse, was in charge of recruitment. His papers contain meticulously compiled hitlists of army officers, clergymen, politicians, literary types – even a society portrait painter (Simon Elwes) and a Polar explorer (Augustine Courtauld). The tone of Luttman-Johnson's letters is deeply serious – in a schoolboyish way – as are the carefully measured replies from his correspondents. There are rare flashes of humour, as when opinions are sought as to an appropriate name for the club. Simplicity should be the keynote, said one correspondent, as in the Fabian Society not being called the "slow progress towards socialism" society. There was the occasional dissenter:

> Bother the 'Roads to Fascism' too. I want your movement to hurry up and put an end to the license of the daily press. It would be glorious to dance on the combined cesspit that holds the dead *Daily Express*, *Daily Chronicle* and *Daily Herald*.
>
> My dictatorship programme would also uproot all telegraph poles and then bury the wires, assume ownership of all the sea-beaches – and scrag the police.
>
> > Yours not very sincerely,
> > T. E. Shaw

In a later and rather less frivolous note to Luttman-Johnson, Lawrence of Arabia gently expressed his lack of confidence in the effectiveness of this or any other secret society. As it turned out, his remarks on how power is really wielded in Britain proved well-founded and stand as a note of caution to anyone who assumes it will be short work to rattle or empty the cage.

> Politics in England mean either violent change (I care not enough for anything to lead me into that) or wasting 20 years of one's time and all one's strength pandering to the House of Commons. The meanest Government servant has more power than any unofficial MP. So I can't afford politics either.

I suppose Mosley is doing his best. He is daemonic, and a leader of conviction...... but the staff work very patchy. Men are only made great by the linked force of their friends. The lesser Elizabethan dramatists made Shakespeare great! If only you had some real opposition. These Jews, Diehards, Liberals are like wet brown paper. What faces you actually is the machine of government; and what ails you is that you don't know where the keyboard is – or so I think.

In addition to the machine of government, there was another problem that hindered nearly everyone wanting to make a difference on the right wing, with the exception of Oswald Mosley. That, of course, was money. Whatever else that can be said for or against it, Fascism is an expensive hobby, requiring uniforms, banners, flags, hired muscle and high-profile venues. In Mosley's HQ in Battersea Park Road there were, at any given time, over 200 men working out, doing gymnastics, training in martial arts. The Leader, if not in his open-topped Bentley, cruised the streets of Chelsea and Mayfair in a fleet of armoured cars, accompanied by a bodyguard of black-shirted 'Biff Boys'. At one point in 1938, Mosley was subsidizing the BUF to the tune of £35,000 a year, which translated into today's terms amounts to thousands of pounds *per week*. Even allowing for the well-documented funding he'd had from Mussolini – and less generous but nonetheless significant contributions that Unity Mitford and Diana Mosley had managed to extract from a disinterested Hitler and a skeptical Goebbels – an exercise like the BUF was a luxury few could afford. Elsewhere, in America, Italy and Germany for example, money was and is still comparatively easy to extort or steal under the plausible cover of some seemingly legitimate and officially endorsed enterprise. In Britain it was by no means easy to raise the wind unless you were a Mosley or a Northcliffe. Thus the pen, the printed word, the old school tie and the war record were the currency tendered in most of the patriotic societies.

Much has been written about Mosley, an excellent introduction to his life and to the BUF being *Mosley* by Nigel

Jones. In it Jones usefully divides the BUF's history into three periods. 'The first, which might be called the "Italian era" lasted from 1932 to late 1934. The second, "the German era", was a trough between two peaks, lasting from late 1934 to 1938. The third and final phase, "the pacifist era", lasted from 1938 until the movement was banned and its leaders interned in 1940.' His many extant portraits and photographs suggest a quite different division of Mosley's life into convenient segments. First we see what looks like a Byronic idealist, in Glyn Philpot's painting in the National Portrait Gallery in London, a dreamy Fitzrovian icon that one might easily suppose to be a poet or a painter. Then there is the bounder, typified by a photograph of Mosley, on the Lido with Cimmie, every inch the matinee idol, recalling the well-known words of Stanley Baldwin, that Mosley was a "cad and a wrong un" – and the prophetic utterance that followed them: "...a cad and a wrong 'un. *And they will find out.*" Following that came Valentino in knuckledusters, Mosley the Blackshirt, inspecting ranks of adoring working-class female Fascists in the north of England. Finally, one glimpses him in late middle age, raising a pint with chorus-line of tipsy East End ruffians. As his son Nicholas put it, 'There was dad on top of a van again and bellowing; so much older now with his grey hair and grey suit. . . there he was roaring on about such things as black men being able to live on tins of cat food, and teenage girls being kept by gangs of blacks in attics. And there were all the clean-faced young men round his van guarding him; and somewhere, I suppose, the fingers of the devotees of the dark god tearing at him.'

Given Mosley's considerable appeal to both men and women and the enormous budget he commanded, it is in some senses odd that he didn't get further in his cause than he did. His failure is often ascribed to hubris. Among Mosley's most loyal and intelligent friends were Bob Boothby and Harold Nicolson, who both in their different ways issued the warning, "remember thou art mortal". In Mosley's early days as an outspoken MP, when he castigated the Government for the brutalities of Ireland, Boothby told him to sit tight, since if he played the game he could expect to be swept to high office in a Churchill government. Lord Lymington, in *A Knot of Roots*, recalls how in 1932 he attended a Conference in Rome when he and Sir Rennell Rodd were invited to a private audience with Mussolini in the Palazzo Venezia. Mussolini's remarks on Mosley are of interest.

> [Mussolini] suddenly turned to me and asked me the most searching questions about the English political scene. It was clear that he was very well informed, and that polite evasions would not get us anywhere. To Rennell's grave disapproval I gave quite frank straightforward answers, upholding my country but not, unless they deserved it, our politicians. I became more than ever struck by his very intimate grasp of the situation. Oswald Mosley came up as the result of a question. "Ah," said the Duce, "he has been spending most of this summer on the French Riviera. I spent quite a lot of time on the Riviera myself, but I was in exile struggling to make a living with my hands. It's not a place for serious reformers to linger in private villas or grand hotels for more than a few days. He wants too much the best of both worlds." This may have been unfair to Mosley as a Fascist leader, I do not know. It was certainly a very shrewd observation from an outside colleague.

There is much to be said for the idea that Mosley was at heart a part-timer, his true spiritual home the Lido, the Riviera or even his bachelor flat in Ebury Street, where he sipped champagne with John Strachey and plotted the seduction of the latest mistress. Ultimately, despite the massive displays at Olympia and Trafalgar Square, the rigours of world domination, not to mention the 'staff work' alluded to by T. E. Lawrence, were too exacting to command his hedonistic spirit.

Regardless of their effectiveness, funding or efficiency, what all the secret societies had in common was an affection for Germany: throughout the Thirties, the mindset of the upper-crust right wing was, if not specifically pro-Nazi, pro-German. The idea was that Germany and Britain had much in common, including 'common sense', a concept so hallowed by Germans that they do not translate it. There was, it was felt, a down-to-earthness about Germany which, masterfully channeled by Hitler, had resulted in an impressive and workmanlike reconstruction of a country left desolate by World War I and further violated by the decadence and cultural pandemonium of the Weimar Republic, a cesspit, many felt, crawling with Jews, Bolsheviks and homosexuals. The French, with their fancy ways, were to be mistrusted. Mussolini was a good sort, to be sure, but Italian. The Germans, though, were more 'like us'. A good Englishman and a good German would, it was instinctively felt, much prefer a solid painting by Carl Spitzweg to some torrid scene by Otto Dix. British and Nazi conservatism sat well together – Hitler's unimpeachable water-colours of Cologne Cathedral would not look out of place in any middle-class British home; Goebbels admired Noel Coward and called for a German version of *Cavalcade*. As Gerwin Strobl memorably put it in *The Germanic Isle*, 'The Third Reich was energized from top to bottom by people who wanted to whistle a recognizable tune after a concert, who liked to be able to tell from a distance whether a painting was hung the right way up or not, and who longed for the return in architecture of pointed roofs, vernacular ruralism, and the Doric order.' Moreover, in an attempt to soften any animosity that might have been left over from the last show, much was done to promote camaraderie between World War I veterans of both sides, an example being the exchange visits organized by the British Legion. Everywhere from Bath to Baden, ran the thinking, good Germans and good Britons wanted peace, order and prosperity – and as war became ever more likely, the efforts of the pro-German lobby became increasingly vigorous. In his 1952 autobiography *The Nameless War*, Ramsay (often described as a deeply religious man) recalled his own interpretation of Mein Kampf and his view of Hitler as a natural friend and ally of Britain.

On the last page and in almost the last paragraph of *Mein Kampf* is the following: 'The party as such stands for positive Christianity, but does not bind itself in the matter of creed to any particular confession. It combats the Jewish materialistic spirit within us and without us.' Looking round the world for help in the battle against this terrible menace of Jew directed Bolshevism, Hitler's mind constantly reverted to Britain and the British Empire. He always longed for their friendship, always declared Britain to be one of the greatest bulwarks against chaos; and that her interests and those of Germany were complementary and not contrary to one another.

Those in favour of doing a deal with Hitler – in favour of Appeasement – found their views articulated and all the options explored in the pages of a significant publication of the late Thirties, the *Anglo-German Review*.

In *The Roots of Appeasement* Martin Gilbert drew a useful distinction between the 'old appeasement' and the 'new'. Whereas the old was 'Victorian in its optimism, Burkean in its belief that societies evolved from bad to good and that progress could only be for the better', the 'new' reflected a 'mood of fear, Hobbesian in its insistence upon swallowing the bad in order to preserve some remnant of the good'. Something of the flavour of both brands comes across very strongly in the *Anglo-German Review*, published between 1936 and 1939, listing several Right Club members amongst its contributors, notably Lord Redesdale and Charles Sarolea – and many others closely connected with Archibald Ramsay, like Barry Domvile who used the *Anglo-German Review* as a mouthpiece for The Link, when that society was still at the fledgling stage. Under C. E. Carroll's editorship, the *A-GR* proclaimed a clear message, a clear sense of purpose and direction. Judged in purely journalistic terms, it was a far greater success than *Action*, the magazine of Mosley's BUF. That, under the fastidious but intensely intellectual supervision of Harold Nicolson, had been an uneasy hotchpotch of sabre-rattling and highbrow, where stirring accounts of the Leader were juxtaposed with helpful gardening tips from Vita Sackville-West. *A-GR*, by contrast, was very sharply focused.

Peace at any cost was its keynote. The tone was upbeat and breezy, calculated as far as possible to appeal to the broadest spectrum of British society. The magazine sought, identified and celebrated common ground between Germany and the United Kingdom, cemented by shared values and aspirations on the one hand and, on the other, values and virtues that each side could offer the other in the spirit of friendship and reconciliation in the wake of World War I. At the outset, the *A-GR* was devoid of anti-Semitism or racism of any other kind, though there were outbreaks, notably in the music columns, where 'negroid jazz' was given a firm thumbs-down. Later on, with war imminent, anti-Semitism crept in, as we shall see.

The advertisements and announcements in *A-GR* give an intriguing picture of Britain in the mid-Thirties, its values and susceptibilities. Modern Touring of Lower Regent Street offered 'Eighteen Days through Germany, Austria and Czechoslovakia for £31, in high-powered luxurious motor cars'; 'The home without a piano lacks one of the greatest sources of pleasure – the capacity for full self-expression: Bluthner: "The Piano with the Golden Tone" '; 'Swastica [sic] Badges, black enamel chromium finish 9d each; Bar gilt brooch, 1/3, post free from T. C. Nobbs, 51 Gorringe Park Avenue, Mitcham'; 'Under the auspices of the Anglo-German Academic Bureau a Company of German Amateur Players presents Friedrich Schiller's "Maria Stuart" (in German) at Battersea Town Hall'. We learn that the All-Hohner Orchestra of the British College of Accordionists toured Germany in the summer of 1939. Events in Germany were prominently listed, the hurly-burly of social and cultural life called vividly to life in a monthly calendar. Readers were alerted to the German Dancing Championships in Kassel and the Exhibition of Degenerate Art in Stuttgart. At the Cologne Dog Show in November 1938, the Führer's Special Prize for Best of Breed was co-adjudicated by Colonel G. G. Woodwark, the Mayordesignate of Kings Lynn. There was even a motoring column contributed by Gordon Fathers, founding father of the laddish lyricism favoured by today's motoring correspondents.

> To the man to whom the smell of racing oil is the most fragrant perfume, the very name Frazer Nash evokes dreams as lotus-like as those of the opium-smoker.

In the October 1938 edition of *A-GR* Fathers performed the impressive journalistic contortion of weaving the Munich Agreement into the motoring review.

> It [the Mercedes-Benz Type 540 Cabriolet] has eight supercharged cylinders, and a four-speed gearbox, all gears being synchronized, and an unusual fifth gear incorporated in the back axle. Although it is a monster of a car it has surprisingly graceful lines. The chassis price is £1,395. Those who have the necessary in the bank could not do better than to take the advice of a famous daily and buy themselves this as a "peace" car.

All of this was intended to create a sense of 'normality', common sense, co-operation; as time wore on, preceding and surrounding the Munich Agreement, the *A-GR* resolutely presented an upbeat picture of Anglo-German friendship, openly chastising the Winston Churchills, Duff Coopers and Anthony Edens for being irresponsible 'warmongers'.

> [Winston Churchill] has committed himself utterly and most emphatically to a power-policy that would lead straight to war. War we might perhaps win – but still, war. Let us pray that no Winston Churchill ever comes to power either in this country or Germany. He is unquestionably the biggest warmonger in the world today.

The *A-GR* line was communicated through an array of contributors, ranging from what would today be called 'lifestyle' journalists through to no-nonsense characters like Redesdale and

Bruce Bairnsfeather or political heavyweights like 'famous historian' Sir Raymond Beazley and the Right Club's Charles Sarolea. Each contributor was trumpeted in a succinct biog in the prelims of the magazine: 'Elizabeth Craig, probably the world's most famous woman journalist' who 'lives at Hampstead in a converted Wesleyan Chapel', 'the last thing in all electric up-to-dateness'. Mrs Craig's piece in Volume 1 Number 1 of *A-GR* was entitled 'The German Housewife' and in it she leaves no doubt as to the lessons a British woman might profitably learn from her opposite number in Germany:

> If I had my way, I would turn every Englishwoman into the equivalent of a German Hausfrau, whether she were married or not. If the average Englishman realized the difference between having his home mismanaged and managed, he would back me up. There is no excuse for slovenly housekeeping any more than there is an excuse for slovenliness in the business world. If more women realized that, we should hear fewer tales of domestic strife. Looking back to the days I spent overlooking the Leitzensee, I wish I had paid closer attention to the example I found in Berlin. Meticulous in every detail appertaining to home comfort, the German housewife sees that her kitchen is efficiently equipped before she begins to think of her personal needs. A fur coat can wait. She does not know the call of a club. Bargain sales do not make her lose her head. In short, the German Frau puts the interests of her household first. I wish I could treat every budding housewife to a year in Germany. Germany is the only country I know where sheer common sense is brought to bear upon the minutest problem of the home.

The article develops further in the same vein and is accompanied by a useful photograph, by way of inspiration, captioned 'Elizabeth Craig, chatting with "Ossi von Stresow", her German Dobermann-Pinscher.'

In its first issue the magazine addresses the vexed issue of dictatorship in Germany. Since dictatorship was a very un-British thing, the *A-GR* felt obliged to offer its readers some plausible justification for the German regime. The task of persuasion fell to Redesdale, described as having a 'broad mind, sound judgment' and a 'sense of humour'; 'a strong, silent man, but not too silent' who 'speaks precisely and well'. In an article entitled 'This Way Lies Peace – A Plea for Better Understanding Between Germany and Britain', he tackled the issue head-on, his irresistible logic combining the elegance of Athens with the briskness of Ascot.

> What ill will does exist here against Germany is due largely to confused thinking.
>
> For instance, there is the man who says "I am deadly opposed to any form of Dictatorship." To him I say, "So am I," but I qualify what I say by adding "...in this country."
>
> What is the sense of a man who is in the enjoyment of good health saying to another who is taking some potent drug and being relieved, if not completely cured, of some ghastly and agonizing disease, "I am opposed to the taking of potent drugs." Obviously, there is no sense in that.
>
> Equally, there is no sense in an Englishman saying to a German that he is opposed to Dictatorship.

Should this line of reasoning have failed to convince, then readers might have considered a more elaborate thesis put forward by Professor Charles Sarolea, a fellow Right Club member, in a later edition of *A-GR*. Scotland, he claimed, was the cradle of Nazi philosophy; Thomas Carlyle, with his mistrust of the ballot box, was the inspiration of the Third Reich. After all, Carlyle had memorably said: 'find in any country the ablest man that exists there; raise him up to the supreme place and loyally reverence him; you have the perfect government for that country; no ballot box, parliamentary eloquence, voting, constitution building, or other machinery whatever can improve a whit'. Sarolea's piece prompted a courteous challenge from south of the border by Professor A. P. Laurie, described by *A-GR* as a 'famous scientist, pedagogue, student of human affairs and Member of the National Council of The Link'. Laurie quoted the following words of the revered English visionary, John Ruskin:

> [the] discipline of the masses has hitherto knit the sinews of battle: a government which shall have its soldiers of the ploughshare as well as its soldiers of the sword, and which shall distribute more proudly its golden crosses of industry – golden as the glow of the harvest – than it now grants its bronze crosses of honour – bronzed with the crimson of blood.

Whilst 'his thought is often confused', said Laurie of Ruskin, 'he is searching in the dark for a dimly visible light; but the germs of National Socialism, including the Labour Camp, and the recognition of the right foundation of the State on blood and soil, are to be found in his writings'. Elsewhere in *A-GR*, we read that a German director had recently completed a film of a play by another advocate of the National Socialist *Weltanschaung*, Oscar Wilde.

If Redesdale was its avuncular voice of common sense, Charles Sarolea provided the intellectual voice of the British right. His views are always expressed with balance and caution, especially so when addressing two contentious topics, one of them Russian Jews, the other the racial and cultural make-up of Poland. On Jews:

> I am quite ready to admit that the Jewish leaders are only a proportionately infinitesimal fraction, even as the British rulers of India are an infinitesimal fraction. But it is none the less true that those few Jewish leaders are the masters of Russia, even as the fifteen hundred Anglo-Indian Civil Servants are the masters of India. For any traveller in Russia to deny such a truth would be would be to deny the evidence of our own senses. When you find that out of a large number of important Foreign Office officials whom you have met, all but two are Jews, you are entitled to say that the Jews are running the Russian Foreign Office.

Regarding Poland, Sarolea articulated more efficiently than most the view that Danzig was 'a purely German town'.

> Ninety-five per cent of the population are Germans. So homogeneous a population is, in itself, sufficient to prove that Danzig always was a purely German town.... Nor, strangely enough, did the Polish people themselves ever try to settle in any large numbers in Danzig territory, so that a Polish minority problem never had any occasion to arise. It is, indeed, a curious anomaly, as was set out ... in a recent article, that after 300 years of personal union under the Polish kings and of close commercial intercourse, a much larger proportion of the Danzig population should have been of Scottish origin than of Polish origin."

Of the more obscure Right Club members, Nancy Brown contributed a travel piece, 'Rhineland Holiday', to the July 1939 issue. This holiday was one of several group tours organized by The Link and had clearly been enjoyed by the writer:

> The sound of children's voices raised in a marching song, while we sat in a beer garden, gay with flowers, shady with sweet-smelling lime trees, watching the ripples on the lake at Marcus Mill. Presently the children came into sight from out of the dark forest, knapsacks on backs, and swarmed into the garden for refreshment. One bright-eyed boy was playing his accordion, and as he played the shining plaits of the little girls around him gleamed in the sunlight like neat braids of gold.

> It appears that every school has by law to take its children on such an excursion at least once a month, and the wisdom of such a step seemed amply justified by their physical perfection and high spirits.

The *A-GR* greeted the Munich Agreement with a series of 'considered statements' by its more prominent contributors, amongst them Ramsay himself and three other Right Club members, the Duke of Wellington, the MP Sir Ernest Bennett and Lord Redesdale. In these statements Neville Chamberlain was feted as hero and saviour, his detractors dismissed as troublemakers and warmongers. Ramsay scrupulously avoided any anti-Bolshevik or anti-Semite overtones in his statement, though seen in the context of utterances he made elsewhere, it is clear who he meant by his descriptions of 'disruptive international forces' which 'seek to build a godless and materialistic hell out of the debris of European civilisation'. Taking a customary swipe at the press, he deplored 'the systematic campaign kept up by international news agencies'. Right Club member Ernest Bennett praised 'the joint efforts of Herr Hitler and Mr Chamberlain' that had 'brought back to Europe that international peace and goodwill which the "men of Versailles" – to quote Field-Marshal Goering's words – had almost "banished from mankind".' He offered a 'word of advice to our German friends':

> If Germans see an insulting cartoon by Low or read abusive and vitriolic speeches by irresponsible English politicians, will they please remember that such exhibitions of malevolence spring to a large extent from mere party prejudice or personal animosities, that there is no machinery for controlling them in a democracy, and that the great mass of our people attach very little importance to them? The vast majority of our countrymen trust the pledge of both the Führer and our own good Prime Minister.

Redesdale was predictably unimpressed that anyone in the country should dare criticize Chamberlain – 'I cannot recover from my amazement...'. The Duke of Wellington hedged his bets.

> In the history of the world it is seldom found that any nation goes to war within fifty years of a great war. And it is very doubtful whether any representative plunging his nation into war would survive doing so, in modern times.

Throughout its 33-issue run, the *A-GR* consistently extolled

Hitler as a dynamic, kind, firm saviour of an embattled nation – a nation with which Britain had for centuries sustained a strong cultural bond. By and large it reiterated Lord Redesdale's opinion of Hitler as a 'right-thinking man of irreproachable sincerity and honesty'. The position of *A-GR* contributors was concisely summed up in The Link's famous 1938 letter to *The Times*.

> Sir, - The undersigned, who believe that real friendship and cooperation between Great Britain and Germany are essential to the establishment of enduring peace not only in Western Europe but throughout the whole world, strongly deprecate the attempt which is being made to sabotage an Anglo-German rapprochement by distorting the facts of the Czechoslovak Agreement. We believe that the Munich Agreement was nothing more than a rectification of one of the most flagrant injustices of the Peace Treaties. It took nothing from Czechoslovakia to which that country could rightfully lay claim and gave nothing to Germany which could have been rightfully withheld. We see in the policy so courageously pursued by the Prime Minister the end of a long period of lost opportunities and the promise of a new era compared to which the tragic years that have gone since the War will seem like a bad dream.
>
> Yours truly,
>
> Arnold, Bernard Acworth, Raymond Beazley, C. E. Carroll, J. Smedley Crooke, W. H. Dawson, Barry Domvile, A. E. R. Dyer, Fairfax of Cameron, Hardinge of Penshurst, Edward Inglefield, F. C. Jarvis, Douglas Jerrold, John Latta, A. P. Laurie, Londonderry, V. B. Molteno, Mount Temple, A. H. M. Ramsay, Wilmot Nicholson, Redesdale, G. Lane-Fox Pitt-Rivers, Arthur Rogers, Arthur Solly-Flood, Nesta Webster, Bernard Wilson.

Until 1937, even after Barry Domvile had established a regular spot as columnist and commentator of The Link, the magazine remained resolutely pro-German rather than anti-Semite in political tone. The first whiff of anti-Semitism came in the August 1938 issue of *A-GR*, which contained an article entitled

'Regrettable Campaign', opening with the following explanation.

> A section of the Jewish community in Great Britain – we believe a small section – is waging a campaign which, though it contrasts sharply with the wise restraint shown by many leaders of British Jewry in their attitude towards Germany, is likely, if it continues, to do infinite damage to all British Jews. For that reason alone it should be discountenanced, for it leads inevitably to the creation of a Jewish question. But we are concerned with it here more especially because of its bearing on Anglo-German understanding.

Leslie and Lewis Lazarus, directors of Lucifer Ltd, manufacturers of boxes of matches and matchbooks, had waged the 'campaign'. The Lazarus brothers, along with many Jewish businessmen in Britain, were dismayed at what had now become the widely publicised persecution of Jews in Germany. They and many others felt that a boycott of German goods would constitute an immediate and effective protest against the regime in Germany. Accordingly, Lucifer Ltd manufactured – 'published' would be an appropriate word – a match-book with the slogan 'Boycott Everything German' printed on the inside cover. A further flourish was evident on the matches themselves, each of which was individually printed in such a way that when the book was open, one was unequivocally invited to 'Boycott' 'Everything' 'German' and 'Buy' 'British'. This simple but effective protest was described in reproachful tones by *A-GR*. Its reaction to the Lucifer matchbook captures exactly the spirit in which an influential cross-section of the British right wing approached any criticism of the Reich's domestic policies regarding Jews.

> Undoubtedly the German Jews are being harshly treated, though the atrocity reports to which so much publicity is given are more often than not quite demonstrably untrue.
>
> On the other hand, the German Government, and the overwhelming majority of the German people, have a strong case

against the Jews. That case is not given publicity in this country, and we have no desire to dwell on it here.

But there is one aspect that does concern us. It is this: We are most emphatically convinced that the charges levelled against the Jews by the German Government and those raised by the Jews against the German Government should not be used to foment discord between German and Britain and thus endanger peace.

Yet that is precisely what is being done. It is being done openly and ruthlessly, even by refugees to whom we are giving hospitality in this country, and all the protection and benefit of our liberal institutions.

We do not know into what category falls the firm of Messrs Lazarus but, if our assumption is correct, those gentlemen are allowing racial prejudice to outweigh their conception of what they owe to the country that harbours them.

So far as the Right Club was concerned, there were, among its members, representatives of every conceivable kind and colour of British anti-Semitism. It was not simply a matter of knee-jerk Jew-hating and Jew-baiting. There was a spectrum of intensity, a confusion of different agendas. Some hated Jews because of the supposed threat Jewish immigrants posed to the livelihood of British workers. Others believed in the theory of a Judaeo-Bolshevik plot. Some thought all successful British Jews from Disraeli onwards to be dangerous and parasitical *arrivistes*. Still others were preoccupied with the dangers that might flow from the contamination of Nordic blood by the 'alien' strain. A few took the single-issue approach, focusing on the supposed barbarities of the kosher method of slaughter. One right-wing group whose anti-Semitism was rather less obviously expressed was the view of what might be termed the "Rural Right" – sometimes called Rural Revivalists – right-wing individuals and groups who saw liberty, wholesomeness and health enshrined in the traditions of the countryside[3]. As Oswald Mosley put it, in support of the Rural Right, "Any civilisation that is to endure requires constant replenishment from the steady, virile stock which is bred in the health, sanity, and natural but arduous labour of the countryside."

The Right Club member most closely aligned with this tradition was the prolific author Anthony Ludovici. He was something of a polymath (having been in early life an artist and an assistant to Rodin) but is notably chiefly as a specialist on Nietzsche and as a champion of Eugenics. Ludovici, whose book *Jews and the Jews in Britain* we shall look at presently, was closely associated with Viscount Lymington, a leading right-wing figure who championed the cause of the Rural Right and who, as proprietor of the right-wing magazine *New Pioneer*, actively encouraged the dissemination of extreme views. Gerald Wallop – Viscount Lymington as he was in the Thirties, before eventually succeeding as the Earl of Portsmouth – was at first glance a fairly run-of-the-mill product of the establishment. After Winchester, Balliol and the Life Guards he was elected Conservative member for Basingstoke. In the early Thirties he met both Hitler and Mussolini. Initially a member of William Sanderson's 'muck and mysticism' organization, the English Mistery, Lymington broke away to found the English Array. This movement, whose founder members included Anthony Ludovici, advocated a return to a traditional agrarian economy. In this new age the very best

---

[3] These right-wing 'Rural Revivalists' organizations are not to be confused with a no less eccentric and interesting rural movement, the Kindred of the Kibbo Kift. This, founded by John Gordon Hargrave, sought to break away from, rather than affirm, the militaristic values upheld in the Scout Movement and, later, in movements like the English Array and the English Mistery. Though their manifesto was gentle, the KKK was not above organized rebellion. For example, until the Public Order Act put paid to uniforms, they wore green shirts and became known as the 'Greenshirts'. KKK members threw a green-painted brick through the window of 11 Downing Street and on one occasion set fire to an effigy of Montagu Norman outside the Bank of England.

produce, for example 'properly manured vegetables', in today's argot 'organic', would be plentifully produced by well-drilled rustics, bringing about nationwide health, vigour, fulfillment and self-sufficiency. The wholesome agenda appealed to a broad spectrum of people including Reginald Dorman-Smith, the Unionist MP for Petersfield and President of the National Farmers Union. But there was a dark side.

Lymington's 1965 autobiography, *A Knot of Roots*, provides an interesting insight into his ideals.

> ...what I want to do here [in Chapter V] is to describe what I might call a school of agricultural philosophers, perhaps I should say ecological thinkers, but no one word can describe the underlying thought and instincts which prompted us in very varying degrees, and gave us as many facets as a rose-cut stone. The underlying thing that brought us together was a deep feeling that "progress" was destroying our minds and bodies in peace as well as war. The more we received a modern education the more spiritually illiterate we were becoming. The more we watched, be it sport, cinema and later television, the less we did. The more we heard the less we listened, the more we ate of preserved and processed foods the less we truly digested.

Lymington goes on to paint an apparently innocuous, albeit somewhat dotty and unworkable, picture of rural self-sufficiency. In Lymington's England,

> Rich land of stout pub-hearty, self-willed people,
> Where lintels lean below the crazy steeple,

genuine tenth-generation rustics, farmers, landowners and livestock breeders labour, dance and drink ale alongside 'doctors and writers, journalists, historians, poets philosophers and politicians'. Anything that smacks of 'progress', e.g. new-fangled machinery, architecture, literature, is to be deeply distrusted. Fresh organic produce, by contrast, is the order of day and a life-giving source of mental and spiritual health. Elsewhere in *A Knot of Roots*, when relating his travels in Africa and India, Lymington speaks warmly of the wisdom that can be gleaned from foreign cultures and brought home, suitably modified, for application in the English rural idyll. Individuals who actively contribute to the pastoral ideal, as opposed to those who passively assimilate its benefits, are warmly praised and upheld as model members of the community.

Rolf Gardiner, forester, musician, farmer and poet, was another of our group. Rolf, because he is leader of his village folk-dancers and the Springhead Ring of singers and youth workers on both sides of the North Sea, was quite wrongly regarded as "whimsy" by some of his more Victorian neighbours. But he breathed life into his village and took away the dullness which far too often characterized rural existence, when it was made up only of whist drives and vicarage fetes as relaxation for its humbler folk. It was and is always a joy to be at Springhead, where Geo Goetsch once said, "They do not live for music but make music part of their lives." Rolf and his wife, Marabel, both lead lives of completely civilized simplicity, but not in the Petit Trianon sense of Marie Antoinette.

Whilst there is no record of how the "humbler folk" took to the enlivenment of their whist drives and fetes by Gardiner's minstrelsy, there is much evidence that there was little Petit Trianon amateurism about his pro-Nazi views – or Lymington's anti-Semitism. Gardiner wondered whether 'the attempt to destroy the Nazi regime, upon which our bellicose idealists are so furiously bent' was worth 'the destruction of Christendom and the setting of an impossible burden upon the shoulders of the blameless youth of the future'. Although Lymington claimed, in the carefully-muted chapters of *Knot of Roots* (it was published in 1965), that

> We [The English Array] did not regard ourselves as Herrenvolk but we wanted our revival to be Anglo-Saxon in the sense that Alfred the Great was Saxon [...]

his utterances in *New Pioneer* some thirty years earlier tell a different story. In those days he had cited *The Alien Menace* by Colonel A. H. Lane, warning that there would be no room in his rural paradise for "the peoples of the ghettoes and the bazaar and the Mediterranean types" who had for too long been debasing the yeoman stock of the northern races. In July 1939 Lymington attacked Government plans to use refugee Jewish labour for agricultural work. British seaports, he said, were 'already an international cocktail of dysgenics' and British land should remain as it always had been, a place 'where indigenous British stock has been kept pure.'

It fell to Right Club member and Lymington associate Anthony Ludovici to raise the stakes and put the case against Jewry once and for all in *Jews, and the Jews in Britain*, published in 1938 and written under the pseudonym 'Cobbett' (a nod to *Rural Rides*, one of the adopted texts of the Rural Right). In one sense Ludovici was a conventional reactionary, while in another he held (and published) some truly disturbing views on race, based on his interest in Eugenics. He began to roll out these views in earnest in *A Defence of Aristocracy: A Text Book for Tories*, first published in 1915 and then republished, after much revision, in 1933. Some of his ideas are unremarkable if considered in isolation. For example, he had the right-winger's time-honoured reverence for Charles I, a ruler who has always attracted a mixed bag of followers. In Ludovici's universe, though, the Caroline persuasion is taken a stage or two further. Charles is held out as an example of one who 'made a stand against the influences and tendencies which ushered in the present Age, *our* Age.' One of the most corrosive of these influences and tendencies was, according to Ludovici, Puritanism, since from the seventeenth century onwards Puritan values had prepared men for the 'shop-counter, the office-stool, the factory and the forge'. This commercialization of the common man had brought about not only an erosion of the delicately balanced agricultural society in which he had thrived for centuries. It had also led, thanks to intolerably unhealthy urban working conditions, to a new breed of malnourished, malcontent and sub-standard Englishman, an underclass: "Look about you now! Observe the myriads of ugly, plain and asymmetrical faces in our streets; observe the illness and botchedness about you." Society, argued Ludovici, was faced with a stark alternative. It could either live with the 'botchedness' in the spirit of fatalistic acceptance practised (he suggests) by Brahmin Hindus – or cut it out with a single stroke of the Eugenist's knife.

> This [Brahmin] valuation of the diseased, the misshapen, the bungled and the botched, is more merciful and more practical than the methods of isolation, segregation and sterilization proposed by the Eugenists; because, if the fact of bungledom and disease is bravely faced by the sound and sick alike, so that they may each feel they are a class apart that must never mix, all compulsory pre-nuptial separations and prohibitions from the quarter of the Eugenist's surgery become superfluous. What is cruel, what is inhuman, is to rear people in the sentimental and quasi-merciful belief that there is nothing "unclean" (the good Old Testament adjective applied to disease) in disease and bungledom, but that a beautiful soul justifies everything; and then, when the world has got into such a state of physical degeneration through this doctrine, to suggest the organization of a pre-nuptial check on all unions contemplated under the influence of this belief, without making any attempt to alter values. But this is just the sort of cruelty that becomes indispensable after too long a spell of sentimental nonsense.

This no-nonsense approach extended to Ludovici's view on the Jews, which he set out in *Jews, and the Jews in Britain*, a book exploring two themes recurrent in Ludovici's thinking. First, a Britain under siege by Jews would face calamity if its native yeoman stock were contaminated with alien blood. Second, social devastation would be inevitable if the unbridled appointment of Jews to high office were to continue (the appointment of the Marquess of Reading as Viceroy of India was held out as an example of how the rot had set in). Ludovici explained what he saw as the difficulties inherent in defining what, in racial terms, a Jew truly is, urging readers not to waste too much time attempting to distinguish between one type of Jew and another.

> For better, for worse, the composite type the Jew presented after the Great Dispersion was his irrevocable destiny. To suggest to a Europe which had learnt to know the Jew intimately only after that event that he is not really a pure type, but a mixture, is like telling a labourer that he cannot regard beer as beer, and cannot deal fairly by it, because he did not know the malt before it was mixed with the hops and glucose, and before it was boiled. He would reply, "I mean beer — not the malt before it was mixed. God alone knows what that was!"

He then went identify the Jewish traits which, he felt, posed the gravest threat to the fabric of British life. Amongst these was his take on the archetype of the 'Wandering Jew', the predatory nomad.

> But the above [characteristics of the Jews], although important, are really less significant for the history of the Jews than are certain other equally strong characteristics which may be inferred from them. We refer to that complex of mental habits, emotions, gifts and tastes which necessarily forms in the nomad State — such, for instance, as the inability to become, or to feel, rooted to any territory, hence the lack of appreciation and capacity for a territorial national's attachment to a particular soil and environment. Such also is the ready ability to become adapted to new surroundings and to a new soil, provided it offers opportunities for a livelihood which are not too offensive to Bedouin or nomad taste. Such, too, is the inability to recognize any obligation to any other man or to any community, in respect of property possessed — in fact, the inability to understand property as a privilege involving responsibilities and duties. The nomad is essentially a particularist who is by nature, as it were, born into the philosophy of the Manchester School, whether this came after or before him. Not only is it difficult for him to

recognize mutuality in the institution of property, but he is also quite incapable of building up a society in which the relations of the various classes and of their members are based on mutuality. He knows only personal property, and when he packs up his household goods and his tent, and moves to a fresh pasture, driving his herd before him, he feels an obligation to no man. He moves, moreover, not merely because he is a rover by nature, but also because he tends, by his congenital disinclination towards productive labour, to exhaust the land on which he establishes his temporary settlement, and his constant refrain, like the essential particularist that he is, is *après moi le déluge!*

Long after the war, in 1955, Ludovici's views remained unaltered, as is revealed in private correspondence regarding the continuing efforts of A. K. Chesterton, in the pages of *Candour*, to encourage anti-Semitism in Britain and South Africa.

> I have not seen a copy of Chesterton's paper for some time, so that I am unable to express any views about its present tone. But my own view is, and long has been, that modern anti-Semitism, including even that of the Nazis, has been precipitate and strategically ill-considered. Before openly attacking a foe so formidable and so safely entrenched all over Western Europe and America, the gathering of forces, the organization of the necessary preliminary propaganda, and the study of the tactics to be employed in the ultimate assault, should all have been accomplished in secret and under cover, until the moment when the Movement was sufficiently powerful and efficient to make success a certainty. To come out too early – i.e. before victory was a foregone conclusion, has simply strengthened the enemy; so that now, all these sporadic little efforts to repeat on a microscopic scale what Hitler failed to do on a gigantic one, are simply laughable, and the enemy must be half-swooning in an excess of hilarity over it all. That is why now, the only wise plan is to start all over again from the beginning; postpone *sine die* the moment for an open attack, and try first of all, year in year out, to discredit the Goi [sic] friends of the major enemy, without mentioning who the enemy is.

This concept of anti-Semitism by stealth, the strategy of discrediting the 'enemy' without mentioning who it is, was widely held in the upper reaches of society. By no means all anti-Semites were so rash as to take the hard line advocated by the likes of Chesterton, Leese and E. H. Cole[4]. A good example of the outwardly 'moderate' type is C. G. Grey, Billy Luttman-Johnson's friend, January Club recruit and editor of the right-wing magazine, *The Aeroplane*. Grey was an extreme anti-Semite, but he took care to define with some precision the particular Jews who, he thought, posed the greatest threat. Broadly speaking, he claimed, he was 'pro-Semitic' – perfectly prepared to acknowledge that the 'Israelitish Jews' had done 'much good work in Germany as in England'. However, whilst maintaining a 'pro-Semitic' position, he was at pains to stress that he was, nevertheless, 'anti-Japhetic'. By this he meant that he was against the Jews he saw as the real menace, the Tartars and the Ashkenazim, descendants of Japheth, immediately distinguishable 'in the Mile End Road' by 'their broad, flat noses, their coarse lips, their high cheek-bones'. His thinking on the Jewish 'problem' and his view on how British Jewry would ultimately bring about its own downfall are clearly set out in a letter to Billy Luttman-Johnson.

> Fanatics like our friend Richard Findlay and my friend George Pitt-Rivers[5] (do you know him?) will always see Jewish influence

---

[4] **Cole, Commander E. H.** Chancellor of the White Knights of Britain, also known as The Hooded Men, who at their clandestine meetings in Lambs Conduit Street swore an oath of allegiance to Edward I. Cole was a leading figure in the Nordic League. He described Israel Sieff as "sitting behind the Government like a huge toad, his loathsome emanations disturbing, misdirecting and jamming every decent impulse that came from the Premier". He referred to Hitler as "that Man of God across the sea, that great Crusader"; believed that "extermination is the only solution to the Jews in Palestine".

[5] **Pitt-Rivers, Captain George Lane-Fox** grandson of General Pitt-Rivers; West Country landowner; Life Member of the Eugenics Society; General Secretary of the International Union for the Scientific Investigation of

behind any policy which does not involve an all-in pogrom. They can never quite see that there is a difference between "Out with the Jews" and "Down with the Jews". I like the old Saxon war-cry "Out! Out!" It is better than the French "*A bas*" The Saxon idea does at any rate give the other chap a chance of getting out of the way.

[Fuller] wrote a splendid book on the Abyssinian War and spoilt its effect by planting a rabidly anti-Jew chapter in the middle of it. If he had kept it for the end people would by then have been convinced of his soundness and foresight.

Yes, Russia does seem to have got rid of the Jew influence. That possibly accounts for the new Greta Garbo film "Ninotchka", which is the most blatant piece of anti-Communist propaganda ever produced on the screen. Which is funny when you consider all the Left Wing propaganda that has been preached in the movies for the past ten years. I suppose the rich Jews are beginning to see that Communism may be a worse danger to them than to anybody else, if it is not run by Jews.

Anyhow whatever they do and whatever we do the people will settle their hash for them sooner or later. Right through history they have always done the same fool trick. They have acquired wealth and then they have become cocky. Then the people have outed them.

For good measure he added, in the valedictory paragraphs of the letter, 'What fun it all is!' In public Grey, and others like him, took a line that has remained current in British right-wing circles to this day, its sentiment being something like 'now look here, some of my best friends are Jews. But…'. One Right Club member was an arch exponent of this line, and his thinking deserves special consideration.

Population; a leading proponent of the idea that Britain was being railroaded into what he called a 'war of racial revenge' by a conspiracy of Bolshevik Jews.

It is easy when considering the Thirties to fall into the trap of thinking that people at large were merely sitting around, rudderless and wracked with anxiety, waiting for the stupendous costume drama of war to happen. Yet on closer inspection, despite the raging of Quentin Bell's 'maelstrom', it becomes clear that there were peculiarly English byways of certainty where, despite everything else that was going on in the world, life went on as usual. One of these was Paultons Square, then as now an agreeable backwater between the Kings Road and Chelsea Embankment near World's End. In July 1937, as the International Brigades embarked on their doomed attempt to break the siege of Madrid and the Foreign Office struggled to find meaning and mileage in the Sino-Japanese War, a letter appeared in *The Times* expressing concern at a proposal that Paultons Square be used as a turnaround point for the new Trolley-Buses. Such a scheme would, said the signatories, endanger the children who used the square; the vibrations of the buses would damage the houses; the erection of overhead cables would destroy the character of the area. "In the belief that the preservation of such squares as Paultons Square is on every ground in the interest of London and Londoners, we desire to add our protest to the protests which residents in the neighbourhood have made against the proposal." What is striking about the letter is not so much the workaday expression of dismay at such an obviously silly proposal, but rather that the Trolley-Bus issue united so many individuals who might otherwise have been at each other's throats, or at the very least somewhat ideologically polarized. The signatories included Max Beerbohm, T. S. Eliot, Henry G. Strauss, Virginia Woolf, E. F. Benson, William Rothenstein, Kenneth Clark, Lord David Cecil, C. E. M. Joad – and Major Francis Yeats-Brown, an avowed and vociferous pro-German and a leading member of Ramsay's Right Club.

Yeats-Brown was the author of *Lives of a Bengal Lancer*, an entertaining and hugely successful book based on his career as a cavalry officer in India. It was made into a film by Paramount, starring Gary Cooper as the 'Yeats-Brown' character, Lieutenant Alan McGregor. Trivia specialists will know that Mohammed Khan, played by Douglas Dumbrille, was the first to utter the line that has since been adapted or misquoted in many other films since: "We have ways of making men talk...". It is less widely known that *Lives of a Bengal Lancer* was Adolf Hitler's favourite film there were many private screenings in his flat in Munich and at his retreat in Berchtesgaden. This film, thought Hitler, exemplified all that was good about England, sterling qualities that in his view the British shared with the Germans. When one looks at some snatches of dialogue it is easy to see why it appealed to him:

> Major Hamilton: [*the men are arguing over Colonel Stone's refusal to disobey orders in order to go after his captured son*] He'll have nothing, if his boy doesn't carry on in this regiment.
>
> Lieutenant Forsythe: Then he'd have everything?
>
> Major Hamilton: Of course he would! That's what it means to him. But d'you think he'd let that make any difference to his orders, to his job?
>
> Lieutenant Alan McGregor: Well, why shouldn't it? Why can't he be a little less of a soldier and more of a man? Why can't he forget his blasted duty for once?
>
> Major Hamilton: Man, you *are* blind! Have you never thought how, for generation after generation here, a handful of men have ordered the lives of 300 million people? It's because he's here, and a few more like him! Men of his breed have *made* British India. Men who put their jobs above everything. He wouldn't let death move him from it. He won't let love move him from it. When his breed of man dies out - that's the end. And it's a better breed of man than any of us will ever make. Good night, gentlemen.

'He wouldn't let death move him from it. He won't let love move him from it.' Here, in Major Hamilton, we see a character in tune not only with the aspirations of the Third Reich (a handful of men ordering the lives of 300 million people) but also recalling sentiments that pre-date Hitler and hark back to the archetypal German hero sung by Ernst Jungers in the wake of Bismarck's imperial ascendancy – the merciless, death-dealing type with *Stahlnaturen* (steely nature), the 'gorgeous bird of prey' who sweeps all considerations of love and death aside. All of this very much chimed with Hitler's view of the world – probably even the peculiarly English concept of heroes as men who 'put their jobs above everything'.

The film was well, if somewhat self-referentially, reviewed in *Das Schwarze Korps*, the official newspaper of the SS. *Lives of a Bengal Lancer* "displays throughout the spirit and conduct which is shared in our new Germany by the entire *Volk*". The review was qualified by open accusations of hypocrisy on the part of British critics of the Nazi regime:

> "They abuse our new Germany abroad, making it out to be one large garrison where drill – and to use their own idiotic terms – 'mindless obedience' suppress and extinguish all humanity; and then from that same world beyond our borders a film reaches us: a scene from the life of a great and powerful nation. A film glorifying precisely that which those vile tongues seek to criticize in us…"

Yeats-Brown became progressively involved in right-wing politics throughout the Thirties. His views, always very elegantly expressed, are set out in his book *European Jungle*, a sort of whistle-stop tour of the Continent in which he airs his thoughts and prejudices on each country in turn – reserving a special chapter for the Jews who, he says, are a talented and industrious nation who would do well if they were to be settled in their own land. For the purposes of this book, his most important utterance was made in July 1939, in the form of an article he wrote for the *New Pioneer* entitled "Listen, Tommy!", addressed to British troops.

This article, containing a mish-mash of pro-Arab sentiment mixed with glowing references to anti-Jewish measures in Germany, ends with the banner headline "Not another British life for Judah". This was the latest angle on Jews: why should Tommy Atkins fight their war for them?

This piece was tame in comparison to the offerings of the more extreme anti-Semites of the Right Club, such as Arnold Spencer Leese and A. K. Chesterton, which we shall examine in due course. It nevertheless came to the attention of Herbert von Dirksen, Ribbentrop's successor as German Ambassador to the Court of St. James, and the last pre-war Ambassador in London. On 19 July 1939 von Dirksen filed an important report to Berlin, summing up for his masters the level and organization of anti-Semite feeling in Britain. It mentions Yeats-Brown and others and begins with von Dirksen's view of the big picture[6].

> If the Marquess of Dufferin and Ava, speaking in the House of Lords on behalf of the Government (July 5 last), not only warns against the growth of anti-Semitism in Britain but even stresses that anti-Semitic feeling has always been a vital and inherent factor in the British nation, this is a fact worth noting. It shows that an appreciation of the Jewish question is also on the increase in Britain. Having regard to the stolid, tolerant racial character of the British, every anti-Semitic impulse must be valued all the more highly, since opportunities for disseminating anti-Jewish ideas are very limited. This fact is already reflected by the suppression of all reports of Mosley's Fascist meetings, which are sometimes very well attended, as well as of the anti-Semitism clashes that occur almost daily in East London.

The Marquess of Dufferin and Ava was the Parliamentary Under-Secretary of State for the Colonies. What he and others actually said in the Lords is quite at variance with the impression that von Dirksen attempts to give of an embattled establishment facing a potentially uncontrollable Jewish 'question'. The speech

---

[6] See Appendix 3 for a full transcript of his despatch to Berlin, p.136.

to which von Dirksen refers followed a three-hour debate in the chamber, initiated by the Earl of Listowel, who wished to call attention to the 'nature and magnitude of the refugee problem created by the political situation in some countries'. The impression one gets from *Hansard* is of a very sophisticated and detailed awareness of the Jewish 'problem', insofar as there was one, as a result of the continuing influx of refugees. The Archbishop of Canterbury, acknowledging the generosity of the Jewish community to the refugees and the benefit that an influx of 'scholars and thinkers and artists' would bestow on the country, reminded the house that it should not forget the plight of children. The Marquess of Reading (a Jew) robustly said that "we do endeavour to bring into this country people who are fit and proper persons to obtain admission to it" and that any increase in anti-Semitism that might result from this would be "very slight" and, in his opinion, "very transient". Lord Harlech dampened further the somewhat half-hearted idea that the Government should sponsor a settlement of Jews in British Guiana:

> Why is there less anti-Semitism here probably than elsewhere, and why is anti-Semitism confined to certain small districts in the East End of London? It is because the Jews have come here and have scattered among the population; they have merged into the general population, and have not lived in a ghetto. Do not let us make any new ghettoes in the new world whether in British Guiana or elsewhere. Let it be a process of infiltration.

Lord Balfour of Burleigh saw refugees as a long-term investment that would eventually repay tenfold its short-term liabilities. This, he felt, was an honest way to look at the problem – after all, we had nearly always profited by being a country of asylum: "...what a double tragedy if not only are we contributing to the tragedy of these unfortunate people who are being condemned to a living death, but at the same time we are refusing to profit by what would be to ourselves an opportunity and a benefit!" Lord Dufferin and Ava, replying to the points raised, said that the "problem of anti-Semitism has, of course, occurred very often before in the history of the world. Usually it has burned itself out fairly quickly, but I do not think that the world has ever witnessed the problem in so vigorous and acute a form as the one in which it presents itself to us today." Their Lordships gave every impression of being ahead of the game and broadly united in trying to find a solution informed as much by basic common sense as it was by an awareness of complicated – and constantly changing – political and economic forces.

Yet despite the measured pace of debate in the Lords, attempts to find such solutions were frequently frustrated by the efforts of small but effective right-wing pressure groups. Here we see instances of the single-issue anti-Semites making some headway, some in the most humane of professions, medicine. Dr Welply, of the 'Medical Practitioners Union', was an associate of Ramsay and Right Club member Aubrey Lees. He wrote a letter, to all Members of Parliament, on the dangers of letting in Czech (Jewish) doctors who lacked British qualifications. Welply and others exerted considerable influence in preventing their very able refugee colleagues from gaining a foothold in the profession in the early days. In his memoirs, *Nine Troubled Years*, Lord Templewood (formerly Sir Samuel Hoare) describes the problem:

> When I attempted to open the door to Austrian doctors and surgeons, I was met by the obstinate resistance of the medical profession. Unmoved by the world-wide reputation of the doctors of Vienna, its representatives, adhering to the strict doctrine of the more rigid trade unionists, assured me that British medicine had nothing to gain from new blood, and much to lose by foreign dilution. It was only after long discussions that I was able to circumvent the opposition and arrange for a strictly limited number of doctors and surgeons to enter the country and practise their profession. I would gladly have admitted the Austrian medical schools *en bloc*. The help these doctors subsequently gave to our war effort, whether in the treatment of wounds, nervous troubles and paralysis, or in the production of penicillin, was soon to prove how great the country's gain from the new

diaspora, and how much greater it might have been if professional interests had not restricted its scope.

At the crudest level, the inner circle of unashamed anti-Semites roundly demonized refugees. Foremost in the circle were two Right Club members, A. K. Chesterton and Arnold Spencer Leese. A. K. Chesterton, an effective speaker, often shared the podium with Ramsay at right-wing meetings. An MI5 agent attended a meeting of the Militant Christian Patriots at Caxton Hall on 23rd May, 1939.

> Captain Ramsay rose to terminate the meeting. We have heard, he said, a most inspiring speech from Mr Chesterton. I am not an apostle of violence, he went on, but the time has arrived for action, and I solemnly state (with slow deliberation) that if our present method fails I will not hesitate to use another. The Jewish menace is a real menace. The time at our disposal is getting short. Take with you, said the Captain dramatically, a resolution in your hearts to remove the Jew menace from our land.

Unlike Anthony Ludovici, Chesterton had few intellectual pretensions. Whilst Ludovici packaged his anti-Semitism as a 'scientific' thesis based on questions of miscegenation, racial purity, disease and so on, Chesterton's was a highly concentrated distillation of racial hatred. He set an unmistakable standard in polemic that very much remains the boilerplate for his ideological successors today. The tone is sufficiently tabloid to be accessible to the vast majority of people – especially when read aloud – yet sufficiently literary to exude an air of authority and stylistic panache: *Mein Kampf* rewritten by Dickens. His pamphlet 'Apotheosis of the Jew: From Ghetto to Park Lane', written and published for the BUF in the Thirties, is typical of a style that was not to change significantly over the succeeding decades of Chesterton's life.

"The Jew arrives in his promised land poverty-stricken and bedraggled. He lives for a time on the smell of an oil-rag while he brings his age-old instincts of the bazaar to bear upon the peddling of old clothes, old bottles, old sacks or whatever it may be until he finds some kind of footing. Thereafter, by means which need not be quoted here, though often they invite closer inspection than the police are able to give them, he is able to replace his rags with a wardrobe of flashy suits and his shuffling gait with a Rolls-Royce car. This is the stage in which he shouts at a British Blackshirt in a British street: "Vy don't you go to Germany? Ve don't want you here!"

After the war, Chesterton set up the League of Empire Loyalists and continued to be regarded as an elder statesman of the right-wing cause. He remained an inspiration, and a unifying spirit, for organizations such as John Bean's British National Party, the Racial Preservation Society and John Tyndall's Greater Britain Movement and Arnold Spencer Leese's heir and ideological successor, Colin Jordan. Chesterton's final significant act on the British political scene was the foundation of the National Front. But, by the seventies, some saw Chesterton's anti-Semite views as outmoded and in need of modification. By now other targets had appeared on the scene, blacks and Pakistanis, to displace Jews in the demonology of the right; Enoch Powell's oratory had stimulated a fresh wave anti-immigrant feeling; the time had come for Chesterton to back down. Nevertheless, he plugged away, as far afield as South Africa, Australia and America, finding and encouraging small pockets of right-wing enthusiasm via his magazine *Candour*.

Arnold Spencer Leese's anti-Semitism was every bit as potent as Chesterton's. High in the demonology of the Right Club and an untiring activist to his dying day, Leese was a veterinary surgeon and, more, a highly respected authority on camels. His book *The One-Humped Camel in Health and Disease* was for the authoritative work on the subject – and even today the book is required reading for those in the field. Richard Bulleit,

Professor of History at Columbia University, makes the following comment on Leese.

> From my particular standpoint as a one-time specialist (and, for want of competition, still an authority) in the history of camel-saddle design, I have often reflected upon a lesson of Leese's career that I saw borne out, in lesser degree, in the lives of certain other camel specialists I learned about in my research: *Do not put too much trust in camel scholars when they stray into areas of important human concern.*

Leese's eternal problem – in effect an inferiority complex to intensify all his other complexities – was that he never really made the grade as Britain's leading fascist. Having founded and single-handedly run the Imperial Fascist League in the twenties, he found himself effortlessly out-run by the young, glamorous, rich and ambitious Oswald Mosley. His relegation to the second desk was a setback from which he never fully recovered. The following extract from Leese's autobiography *Out of Step: Events in the Two Lives of an Anti-Jewish Camel Doctor*, gives a disturbing picture of the relentless and slightly unhinged tenor of his beliefs.

> Let me close this record, however, on an animal note. After the loss of my St. Bernard, and after my first anti-Jewish conviction in 1936, I decided not to acquire another dog. I foresaw that the Jews would try and get me back into prison, in which case I felt that to have a dog at home would add to my own distress in prison, and would not be fair on the dog. But, in 1935, we adopted a ginger male kitten, and Nandy II has been a constant source of entertainment to us for over 15 years; it was through him that I became aware of a sense which some animals (of species not too far removed from the feral) possess which gives them some sort of radar-like warning, presumably vague, of coming calamity. It may be that some humans of primitive type may share this sense with them. As has been narrated, I was arrested in 1940 under 18B and taken away for over three years; and in 1947, I was imprisoned for eight months. During the two

days before these events, Nandy would hardly leave me; he followed me about all over the house and garden, and it was so marked that on the second of these occasions, my wife became convinced that I was in for a stiff term of imprisonment. Nandy was right both times! It is all the more interesting to record that in 1950, when the Government tried to silence me by a criminal libel charge, Nandy took no special notice of me when I departed for the Old Bailey; and this actually gave us some encouragement! And he was right again, because I was acquitted; he was about the only one who expected that result! As I write, he sleeps, soundly, beside me; in his 16th year, not just a Cat, but One of Us!

At about the time of Nandy's adoption, Leese was running the Imperial Fascist League and its newspaper, *The Fascist*, from premises at 33 Craven Street, WC1. "It must be admitted" he wrote, "that the most certain and most permanent way of disposing of the Jews would be to exterminate them by some humane method such as the lethal chamber."

Leese had a burning single-issue, the question of Jewish ritual slaughter. He sensed enormous mileage in the perennial British loathing for cruelty to animals and as a highly respected veterinary surgeon he was ideally placed to exploit it. He published a pamphlet entitled 'The Legalised Cruelty of Shechita – the Jewish method of Cattle Slaughter'. In it he proposed an ingenious strategy for having ritual slaughter banned under the Slaughter of Animals Act 1933, but ultimately the issue was seen as so unsavoury that Leese's public simply lost interest. The debate about slaughter, ritual or otherwise, is one from which no group emerged a winner at the time, the issues ironically proving too distressing for a nation of animal lovers to face. Was it more acceptable to cut an animal's throat and let it bleed slowly to death (the Jewish method) or to hit it on the head with a large mallet or pole-axe (the old-fashioned Gentile method)? Was it better to dispense with traditional methods and fit the animal with a steel slaughtering mask that would protect its eyes and nose and kill it cleanly with a powerful internal spring-loaded bolt? Other right-wing groups were preoccupied with the ritual slaughter too, but none made much of an impact. Among them were the Anti-Vivisection Society, the Animal Defence Society, and the 'Lady Alexandra Hardinge group'. The last of these organized screenings of a gruesome documentary film on Schechita.

In his report to Berlin, von Dirksen observed that 'Anti-Semitic opinions... also find outlet in a section of the English Catholic press, though only insofar as they reveal Jewish connections with Bolshevism, which is violently attacked in Catholic newspapers.' One associate of Ramsay's and of many other Right Club members was Douglas Jerrold, editor of *The English Review*, described by Richard Griffiths as a 'romantic capitalist Catholic in the Chestertonian tradition' (Griffiths means in the tradition of G. K. rather his second cousin A. K. Chesterton). Whilst Jerrold took the conventional Catholic anti-Bolshevik line, he also suggested that right-wing visionaries should mount what came over as a somewhat quixotic challenge to British capitalism. The idea was to unseat the fat cat financiers at one end of the scale and purge the trades unionists and bureaucrats on the other. The latter he dismissed as parasites eager to 'plant themselves securely on the ratepayers back under the pleas of public service'.

More than anything else, it was the Spanish Civil War that polarised British Christians of all denominations. Sir Henry Page Croft thought Franco 'a gallant Christian gentleman', a view supported at the highest level in British society not just by Catholics (Father Francis Woodlock SJ, Arnold Lunn and Sir Charles Petrie) but also by senior members of the Church of England including, for a time, Dean Inge. A dissenting voice, that of A. S. Duncan-Jones, the Dean of Chichester, tried very sensibly to make the point that the Republicans were not so much anti-Christian as anti-clerical. This was too nice a distinction, and was shouted down by the pro-Franco lobby, intent on presenting the Nationalist cause as a crusade. Another aspect of the Spanish

War, which was to weigh increasingly heavy on the consciences of British Christians, was the unignorable part played by the Third Reich. Spain had given the Reich a convenient testing ground for Nazi military muscle – and its successes were exploited to the full by a triumphalist propaganda machine. For example, in October 1937, the Duke and Duchess of Windsor visited Munich where, after visiting the Temples of Honour containing the bodies of the 16 Nazis who fell in the 1923 Putsch, they were 'shown over the House of German Art and saw among other pictures a recent addition to the collection, a painting by Herr Claus Bergen depicting the bombardment of Almeria by the German battleship Admiral Scheer (*The Times*, October 25 1937).

In Paul Collins' *God's New man: The Election of Benedict XVI and the Legacy of John Paul II*, there is a helpful summary of the Catholic position.

> The great fear of Catholics was not of the right but of the left, of Bolshevism rather than fascism. What is also significant is that Jews were often linked to the Left. Catholics in the Thirties were conventionally anti-Jewish rather than anti-Semitic. Religious anti-Judaism is not the same as racial anti-Semitism, but it does create an ambience in which racism can flourish. After all, Catholics were still praying for the 'perfidious Jews' who had executed Jesus as late as 1956 in the Good Friday liturgy. In the Thirties the Jews were incorrectly identified by right-wing Catholics as proponents of secular liberal values that were thought to undermine the identification of Catholicism with European culture. Secular liberalism was seen as the product of a 'Masonic Jewish alliance' and the myth of Jewish world financial dominance was often mentioned. Jews were also cast in the role of leaders of socialism and communism, even though the vast majority of European Jews were actually poor, conservative and orthodox. But these caricatures deeply infiltrated Catholic consciousness. Linked with the Bolsheviks, the Jews were seen as setting out to destroy Christian civilization. The Nazis were easily able to exploit these presumptions.

The Church of England – according to Hitler you could always 'rely on' the Church of England – was cautious, and at times seemingly naïve in its initial response to Nazi persecution of Jews. Archbishop Temple, with the Master of Balliol and others, sent a closely reasoned letter to Hitler deploring the internment of Jews in concentration camps. This, predictably, had no effect whatsoever – and that it was written and sent at all speaks much of how out of touch certain quarters of the Church of England were at the time. It fell to the gadflies to speak out, and none was more outspoken than Herbert Hensley Henson, the Archbishop of Durham.

Henson had an impressive track record as a cage rattler. He denounced, impressively enough from the pulpit of Westminster Abbey, the British directors of the Putmayo Rubber Company for their part in the brutal treatment of Peruvian labourers. From 1935 he railed vigorously at the British Government's acceptance of Mussolini's invasion of Abyssinia. In the Lords, in May 1938, he described Lord Halifax's abandonment of Abyssinia as "the cold sophistry of a cynical opportunism". In July that year, addressing a British Legion rally in Durham, Henson spoke about the 'shocking scandal of anti-Semitism', saying that it sprang from

> two sources, the vicious nationalism of the State and the profound ignorance of the people. We have more Jews in England in proportion to our population than the Germans have in proportion to theirs, and when we are told that this dreadful minority – less than one per cent of the population – is strangle-holding the whole life of the community we say unhesitatingly, "you are talking nonsense." The Jews are like other people – some are capitalists and some are Communists – and if you want to make them all Communists you had better oppress them. Anti-Semitism is a vicious thing, and, unless the British Legion and other citizens are on the watch against it, it may grow up here and lead our free country into the most shocking excess of injustice.

As is so often the case throughout the history of Christendom, the struggles of the individual are more eloquent than the deliberations groups. Dietrich Bonhoeffer's lonely ministry in London in the Thirties, his friendship with the Bishop George Bell of Chichester and his eventual martyrdom in Nazi Germany may well be remembered long after the cautious deliberations of Inge and Temple are forgotten.

For every Right Club member whose views were readily identifiable, there were inevitably others of whom it may be said, rightly or wrongly in the time-honoured defence run by war criminals, that theylqalqlqalqa 'didn't know what was going on'. Three Right Club members illustrate this problem. Two were Conservative MPs, Sir Peter Agnew and Sir James Edmondson. Agnew's blind spot was Romania, Edmondson's Spain. The third was a soldier, Prince Yurka Galitzine, who from an initial position of ignorance about nearly all the issues of the day, embarked on a singular voyage of redemption that brought him face to face with the worst horrors of the war.

Edmondson was involved in a campaign to repatriate Basque child refugees who had found refuge in England in the wake of the Spanish Civil War. These children, some 3,840 of them, had been shipped to Southampton after the fall of Bilbao at the instigation of an all-party committee for Spanish relief headed by the staunch anti-Fascist (and anti-Appeasement) Liberal MP, Wilfred Roberts. Many of these children had been separated from their parents and most of them were too young to understand the intricacies of the situation in Spain. All of them became the victims of an unseemly tug of war between the Children's Committee (their pro-Republican guardians in Britain) and the Spanish Children's Repatriation Committee (a pro-Franco organization chaired by Right Club Warden the Duke of Wellington and supported by the Catholic Church in the person of Cardinal Hinsley). On the one hand the Children's Committee warned that ill-considered and indiscriminate repatriation might well leave the children open to vicious reprisals by Nationalist forces in Spain. On the other, Lady Londonderry warned that the children were being turned into "Christ-hating little Communists" and the right-wing press attributed a crime-wave of car theft and burglary to Spanish juvenile delinquents. In the midst of this, local communities all over Britain gave the children a warm welcome and tried their best to make them feel at home. When they left, there were painful goodbyes, some of them permanent.

Agnew served in the Royal Navy, was Conservative MP for Camborne in Cornwall from 1931-1950 and was in later life a Trustee of The Historic Churches Preservation Trust. He was described in his *Daily Telegraph* obituary as "something of a right-winger, perhaps out of naivety rather than conviction." Richard Griffiths suggests that his connection with the Right Club "is likely to have been based on naivety coupled with knee-jerk right-wing reactions". Agnew, like Ramsay, supported Franco's cause in Spain; he was also pro-German and an active member of the Anglo-German Fellowship. One of his main preoccupations, one shared by Ramsay, Edward Doran and J. J. Stourton, was the influx into Britain of Jewish immigrants and the ease with which they were able to obtain naturalization. Yet it was on another issue that he aired a distinctly dubious view, expressed in the House of Commons in 1932, that questions on the fate of Jews in Romania were "a waste of money". This was said at a time when Romanian Jews were being persecuted by the Legion of the Archangel Michael, widely known as the "Iron Guard" and also known as the "Greenshirts", a clerical-fascist movement founded in 1927 by Corneliu Zelea Codreanu. The Iron Guard, which blended hard-line militarism with Romanian Orthodoxy, is an important example of an anti-Semitic movement that flourished independently of Nazism but was no less extreme. During the Second World War, it played a significant part in the Holocaust. In January 1941, during a three-day civil war in Romania, the

Iron Guard massacred dozens of Jewish civilians in the Bucharest slaughterhouse, hanging the bodies on meathooks in a parody of the Jewish method of ritual slaughter. Codreanu was a charismatic leader. He had developed a catch-all image and ideology for the Iron Guard that involved the usual fascist props of uniforms, rallies and military bands. The ideology rested on a comprehensive selection of perceived threats to Christendom including Judaism, Freemasonry, Freudianism, Marxism, Bolshevism, atheism and homosexuality. The contemporary ideological successor of the Iron Guard in Romania is Noua Dreapta, the "New Right", an organization that reveres Codreanu's memory, is devoted to the restoration of Romania's pre-War territories and is opposed to a wide range of things including the Roma people, The European Union, Mormons and Valentine's Day.

Finally there is the curious case of Prince Yuri 'Yurka' Galitzine. Yurka Galitzine was one of a cluster of young officers who were attracted to the cloak and dagger business of the Right Club. The young naval officer Lord Ronald Graham, an indefatigable party-goer on the right-wing scene, seems to have been the magnet and ringleader of this youthful set. There are other young bucks, such as David Scrymgeour-Wedderburn of the Scots Guards, soon to be killed at Anzio in 1944 aged only 31. Galitzine's name is down in the ledger alongside that of Colin Dennistoun Sword, a lieutenant in the Gordons who was shortly to marry Galitzine's half-sister Pauline Daubeny, also a Right Club member. The recruitment of these young officers was part and parcel of one of Ramsay's stated objectives, to disseminate Right Club values in the armed forces. He realized that instead of recruiting officers of his own generation, preaching to the converted, a more effective strategy would be to recruit young men at the beginning of their military careers. If, as it is reasonable to suppose, Ramsay really believed that one day it would be possible to stage a Fascist military coup, then loyalty in these quarters would be essential.

Galitzine's war diary, a meticulously compiled scrapbook of photographs, tickets, press-cuttings, explanatory notes, references to girlfriends, his own and other people's, cars, planes, trips, dances. It is an optimistic, cheerful document, punctuated only by darker inclusions as the years wear on. Dennistoun Sword is captured and taken prisoner. Other friends are wounded, killed or simply missing. After the war, Galitzine was attached to a war crimes investigation unit, which we shall look at in due course.

Towards the end of the war, he was remembered by an American officer, Alfred de Garcia, also attached to SHAEF, the allied high command in Europe: "Captain Galitzine, handsome and humane, somehow detaches himself and even gets back to England to get married, but then returns like an eel to the Sargasso Sea, very much alive and smiling. He has smashing pictures of the High Society wedding and articles from the Press." Later, de Garzia tells of Galitzine's increasing disillusionment at the day-to-day barbarities of the war.

> [Galitzine] had just been to a trial of militiamen and was upset about the proceedings. A number of youths had been tried and, without the taking of a great deal of evidence and without much formality, they had been sentenced to death. The main fact that was brought out in court was that they were members of the Pétain militia. I remarked to him that I was glad that the FFI had already taken matters into their hands and were dispensing speedy justice. He protested, however, saying that, though he had nothing against the death penalty for traitors, these were mere boys who didn't know what they were doing and who had not committed any atrocity that was proven or done any real harm. They were just small fry. He thought the justice was too summary. I replied that I had no illusions about the individual justice being meted out. Perhaps their delinquency was more a matter of their environment than sheer will on their part. Undoubtedly, those more guilty would escape in large numbers. But who is responsible for anything in this world that he is brought into, warped, according to, and punished for? No eternal law justifies punishment. It is a social act that people often

indulge in to expiate their own sins of thought and deed as much as to protect themselves from the criminal in the future. Galitzine didn't agree. He felt the sentence and the weakness of the convicts as a blow to his innards, a threat to his personal integrity, so great is the myth of personal responsibility, and so great the revulsion against punishment as a social policy (though it has always been unknowingly that).

In the last weeks of the war, Galitzine drafted an ambitious document for circulation amongst the allies, a proposal for an International Bureau of Information. The laudable objective of the agency was to share information and, by doing so, scotch the attempts of dark forces in their bid for global domination. Information would be, as it were, a weapon for peace, and the subscribing nations would effectively play the propagandists at their own game. Describing the project in a letter to *The Times* (11 October 1945), Galitzine wrote that "Few people realise the part propaganda has played in this war and even in the last war. It might well be said that Germany declared war on the world in 1933 when Hitler launched his propaganda offensive against civilization, and it is certain that the measure of success he achieved was in the main due to the influencing of public opinion, especially in undermining the unity of his victims by propaganda."

It was Galitzine's experiences as a war crime investigator that left the deepest impression of all. He was sent as part of a three-man team to investigate Natzweiler, a notorious camp. In *Flames in the Field*, Rita Kramer tells us that

> Yurka Galitzine ... made a number of discoveries. He found all of the camp records intact in the administration building; he heard that there had been some British men in the camp and that some women described as well-dressed spies had been brought there, and he carefully put together a record of the systematic shootings, hangings and gassings, the medical experiments carried out on live prisoners, the conditions of slave labor on starvation rations, the brutal punishments randomly inflicted by

sadistic criminals put in charge of the barracks, and other details of daily life in the camps that had been intended to pave the way for the New Order promised by the Third Reich. No one would believe him. Galitzine had 'heard' about the atrocities in the camp from four escaped prisoners who gave him a tour of the abandoned camp.

Galitzine's report – and the photographs that accompany it – speak for themselves.

The SS men conducting the interrogation were given wine and spirits to whip-up their fury still further, and afterwards, knew no restraints. The prisoners in the next room could not sleep during the night because of the continuous cries of pain of those being tortured. At reveille, the accused were taken away. Most of them had been tortured to such an extent that they were entirely beyond recognition. After four weeks, during which time they continued to have their hands tied to their backs and were exposed to the weather, those concerned were publicly hung, in the presence of all the prisoners. Those chained in this manner had remained chained at all times, and their hands were not free when they had to relieve themselves, or to eat and drink. The chains grew into their flesh, the upper arms were blue from the stopped blood, and had (so to speak) died off.[7]

This traumatic end to Galitzine's war is a fitting point at which to leave this overview of the Right Club. Of all Right Club members, perhaps none travelled further than Galitzine did from the seemingly harmless and exciting spirit of an 'eccentric' British secret society in South Kensington. Certainly none came closer than he did, at Natzweiler, to the brutal consequences of extremism.

---

[7] He adds that 'The ones responsible for this act were SS Hauptsturmführer Kramer, SS Oberscharführer Buttner, SS Hauptscharführer Zeuss, SS Oberscharführer Nietsch, SS Unterscharführer Ehrmanntraut, SS Unterscharführer Fusch, SS Totenführer Ohler'.

The Red Book

In the following pages we reproduce the Red Book list alongside transcriptions of Ramsay's often somewhat erratic entries, together with the full names and ranks where applicable of the Right Club members.

The Red Book itself is a substantial ledger bound in burgundy calf with marble endpapers and gold tooling on the inside borders of the covers. The ledger is manufactured by the leading publishers and stationers, Waterlow & Sons Limited. Their name and the title 'Private Ledger' appear on the spine. The lock is by the well-known makers Bramah of London and shows visible signs of having been broken open following the raid on Tyler Kent's flat in May 1940. The folios consist of an alphabetical preliminary section followed by 193 double page spreads for double-entry book-keeping.

The overall size of the ledger is 10 ¾ inches x 8 ¼ inches x 1 ½ inches and it weighs 5lbs pounds 7½ oz. The top edges of the spine are rubbed and bumped and the front and back covers are pitted and scarred.

Male members of the Right Club are listed on folios 1, 2 and 3. Female members are listed on folios 21 and 22. Names are accompanied by administrative details such as the amount and frequency of subscriptions and contributions, the status of members within the organisation (whether Warden or Steward). Members from Scotland are denoted by the letter 'S' in red. Two Americans have the letters 'USA' in red and one German a 'G' in red. Receipt of the Club Badge is confirmed by a tick, as is receipt of the Membership Card.

Folio 181 contains a list of Stewards; Folio 185 contains a list of members who are MPs; Folio 187 contains a list of Speakers and Writers. There is an addendum in the form of a loose sheet of ledger paper on which there are three groups of names, headed YS, L1 and L2 respectively.

Additional interleaved documents are also reproduced here.

		W		S	Y	K	Badge	Received £ — S — d				Promised Yearly £ — S — d		
S	×	Lord Carnegie					✓	5	.	/		5	.	.
S	×	Lord Colum Stuart MP					✓							
c S	×	Lord Sempill					✓							
	×	John Bailey Esq					✓	41	15	.		10	10	.
S	×	Sir Alexander Walker					✓	100	.	.				
		Harold Mitchell Esq MP					✓							
	×	Peter Agnew MP					✓	5	.	.		5	.	.
	×	Joyce Hw					✓							
		Richard Findlay Esq	×		×	✓		10	6		✓	10	6	
		John Vannck	×			✓					✓			
		Antony Ladoiri				✓					✓			
		Featherstone Hannond C.	×			✓					✓			
		Alex r M Ramsay				✓		2	6		✓			
		Robert M Ramsay				✓		2	6		✓			
		Geary M Ramsay				✓		2	6		✓			
	×	E H Cole				✓		2	6		✓			
		O C Gilbert	×			✓		2	6		✓			
	×	H C Cross Esqr				✓		10	10		✓	10	10	.
		C Scrutauld Skelb				✓		2	6		✓			
		Lees				✓		2	6		✓			
		Capt Collier	×		.	✓		2	6		✓			
		Reavely Cuthert	×			✓					✓			
		M' Cooper				✓								
.	×	Joyce w				✓		5	.					
		Lee G W	×	×		✓					✓			
												31	10	6

Lord Carnegie (Lord Charles Alexander Carnegie, later 11th Earl of Southesk)
Lord Colum-Stuart MP (Lord Colum Crichton-Stuart MP)
Lord Sempill (Col. William Forbes-Sempill, 19th Baron Sempill)
John Bailey (John Bailey, later 2nd Baronet)
Sir Alexander Walker
Harold Mitchell MP (Col. Harold P. Mitchell MP)
Peter Agnew MP (Lt-Commander Sir Peter Garnett Agnew MP)
Joyce Wm (William Joyce)
Richard Findley Esq (Richard Fitzgerald Findlay)
John Vannek (John Vaneck)
Antony Ludovici (Anthony Mario Ludovici)
Featherstone-Hammond C (C. Featherstone-Hammond)
Alex M Ramsay (Alexander 'Alec' Maule Ramsay)
Robert M Ramsay (Robert Maule Ramsay)
George M Ramsay (George Maule Ramsay)
E H Cole (Commander E. H. Cole)
O C Gilbert (Oliver Conway Gilbert)
C Cross Esq (John Carlton Cross)
C Serrocold Skeels (Professor Cecil Serocold Skeels)
Lees (Aubrey Lees)
Capt Collier (Capt. Vincent Collier, a.k.a. 'Hawke' and 'Captain X')
Reavely, Cuthbert (Cuthbert Reaveley)
Mr Cooper
Joyce Wm (William Joyce) <repeated - see above>
Lee G W (G. W. Lee)

	W		S	Y	K	Badge	Received £ — s — d		Promised Yearly £ — s — d
		×	Dr Mellotte						
			Alex Walker	×	✓	1	1 0		1 1 -
S	30		Trooper T. Hunter MP ×		✓		2 6	✓	2 6
		×	George Drummond						
	20	×	Sir J. Edmondston MP						
			Lord Ronald Graham ×		✓		2 6	✓	
			Mjr Ashford		✓		2 6	✓	
			John Beattie		✓		2 6	✓	
		×	The Duke of Wellington						
			Arthur Loveday		✓		2 6	✓	2 6
			A K Chesterton		✓		2 6		
			A Dalrymple		✓				
			J Rushbrook ×		✓		2 6	✓	
			Agassiz Mjr E—		✓			✓	
	40		Mjr Beckett Holmes A		✓			✓	
			Barker Jones 2N		✓			M ✓	
			Mills MT ×		✓			✓	
			Longhurst M B ×		✓			✓	
			Munro E Brooke S.M		✓			✓	
			O'Higgins Mjr		✓			✓	
			Brook S Harwich		✓			✓	
			Button Cpt Mjr		✓				
			Mitchell J		✓			R. & payers	
S		"	Lutman · Johnson H ×		✓			Newton 245	
			Fuller EA		✓				
S	50	"	Sir Samuel Chapman MP ×		✓		S		

Dr Mellotte (Dr James Henry Mellotte)

Alan Walker

Provost T Hunter MP (Provost Thomas Hunter MP)

George Drummond (Captain George Henry Drummond)

Sir J Edmonton MP (Sir Albert James Edmondson MP)

Lord Ronald Graham (Lord Ronald Malise Hamilton Graham)

John Beatty

The Duke of Wellington (Arthur Charles Wellesley, 5th Duke of Wellington)

Arthur Loveday

A K Chesterton (Arthur Kenneth Chesterton)

A Dalrymple (A. D. Dalrymple)

J Rushbrook (J. F. Rushbrook)

Jones N (N. Jones)

Mills HT (Herbert T. V. 'Bertie' Mills)

Longhurst M B (M. B. Longhurst)

Munro E (E. Munro)

O'Higgins

Booth, Dr Meyrick (Dr. Meyrick Booth)

Mitchell J (John Mitchell)

Luttman-Johnson H (H. W. 'Billy' Luttman-Johnson)

Fuller E A (E. A. Fuller)

Sir Samuel Chapman MP

2

Yearly

			Bdy	L	s	d		aw			
	51	Sharpe Rev G.C.		✓				NL	✓		
		Clarke. Richard		✓				IFL	✓		
		Eckersley S.P		✓				(Lt BBC)	✓		
		Powrall George		✓				BU	✓		
		Rowe TWY		✓				NL	✓		
		Kathleen Symonds		✓				NL	✓		
25/5		Bennett. Geoffrey		✓				MCP	✓		
19/5		Holmes. A		✓				MCP	✓		
		Hughes J (Capt)		✓		10		R	✓		
	60	Major J. Egerton	/	/	✓				✓		
		Fitzpatrick Lewis Capt J.	/	/	✓				✓	/	/	0
		Applegate . A.J.		10	6	✓			✓	10	6
	W	Low Rodesdale	/	/	✓				✓	/	/	0
		Somers Capt.	/	/					✓	/	/	0
		Phillip Brocklehurst	/	/	✓				✓			
	S	Todd A.K.		10	6	✓			✓			
		Geo Wingate	/	/	✓				✓	/	/	0
		Bennet Sir E. MP	/	/	✓		MP		✓	/	/	0
		Cook. A.C.			✓							
	70	Corbett E.S.			✓							
		Duncan Alan			✓							
		Down Capt J			✓							
		Eddis Lt Col L.A			✓							
		Foster J.P.			✓							
	75	Graham R. (Nat)			✓							

Sharpe Rev G C (Revd. George Coverdale-Sharpe)
Clarke, Richard (Richard Clarke)
Eckersley PP (Peter Pendleton Eckersley)
Pownall George (George Pownall)
Rowe T W Y (T. W. Victor Rowe)
Kathlee Symonds
Bennett Geoffrey (Geoffrey Bennett)
Holmes A (A. Holmes)
Hughes Capt J (Captain James McGuirk Hughes, alias 'P. G. Taylor')
Major J Egerton
Fitzpatrick Lewis, Capt J (Capt. J. Fitzpatrick Lewis)
Applegate A J (A. J. Applegate)
Lord Redesdale (Redesdale, David Bertram Ogilvy Freeman-Mitford, 2nd Baron)
Somers Capt (Captain Somers)
Philip Brocklehurst
Tod A K (A. K. Tod)
Geo Wingate (George Wingate)
Bennet Sir E MP (Sir Ernest Nathaniel Bennett MP)
Cork A C (A. C. Cork)
Corbett E S (E. S. Corbett)
Devereaux, Alan (Alan Devereaux)
Down Capt J (Captain J. Down)
Eddis Lt Col L A (Lt-Col. Bruce Lindsay Eddis DSO)
Foster J P (J. P. Foster)

			S	K	Y	F			
		Laurence Walter B							
		Lentaigne R.							
		Norris. John							
		Sellig. W.K.							
80		Stokes R.							
		Temple J.							
		Staunton Jtn J MP					Wadhurst 279. Camden Hill. Wadhurst Sussex		
S		Mackie J. MP				MP			
S	(W)	Cowan. Alex Esq	5	-	-				
S		Borthwick. Henry							
		Housfield Jas Esq	1	1					
		Aoratoun Swood J.C.		10	6				
		Galitzine Prince Nicho							
		Brooke. Harold		1	1				
90		Roberts E A Esq				M			
		Carlton. John							
		Bennett Sir E MP		1	1				
S	W	Galloway Earl of							
		Graham F.J.G	1	1				1	1
		Le P. Trench. B.							
		Baker A Baker			e				
		Johnson Coln.							
S		Prior R.	5	-					
S		Weddurburn David S		5		Whi 2715. Que Whi 4104			
						13 Cowley St.			
		Cox. Thos							
100		Hollyer. L.J.				132			

Lawrence Walter B (Walter B. Lawrence)
Lentayne B (B. Lentayne)
Norris John (John Norris)
Seelig W K (W. K Seelig)
Stokes R (R. Stokes)
Temple J (J. Temple)
Stourton Hon J JP (Hon. John Joseph Stourton MP JP)
Mackie J MP (John Hamilton McKie MP)
Cowan Alec (Alec Cowan)
Borthwick, Harry (Brig-Gen. Francis Henry Borthwick DSO CMG)
Horsefield Jn Esq (John Horsefield)
Deniston-Sword J C (Lt. J. C. Dennistoun Sword)
Galitzine Prince Yurka (Prince Yuri (Yurka) Nikolaievitch Galitzine)
Brooke Harold (Harold Brooke)
Roberts E A Esq (E. A. Roberts)
Cannton John (John Cannton)
Galloway Earl of (Randolph Algernon Ronald Stewart, 12th Earl of Galloway)
Graham FJG (F. J. G. Graham)
Le P Trench, B (Wiliam Francis Brinsley Le Poer Trench, later 8th Earl of Clancarty
Prior, R (R. Prior)
Wedderburn, David (David Wedderburn)
Cox, Thos (Thomas Cox)
Hollyce L J (L. J. Hollyce)

3

	101	Kennedy Rev A.J.			✓				
		Lane A.D			✓	M			
		Lane D R			✓	M			
		Lazenby J.G			✓	M			
		Miller A.J			✓	M			
		Paine A.J			✓	RAF			
		Procter A			✓	M			
		Robertson A.M.			✓	M			
		Sykes Victor J.			✓	M			
	110	Thom Ed.F.			✓	RF			
		Thompson, T H			✓	M			
		Walter E.H.			✓	M			
		Thompson Col. H.S			✓	RF			
		Spencer Col Richard			✓	R			
USA		Dulling Aleunt H			✓	R			
		Green C.H.			✓	RAF			
S		Muirhead Jas	N		✓	R			
S		Crawford Tho.		S	✓	A			
S		Inches R.C.			✓	J?			
S	120	Ainslie Tait D			✓	J?			
S		Bree J.P			✓	J?			
S		Shipman		S	✓				
		Wardlaw Ramsay B			10/-	✓	A	L.D	
		Foster P.C.				✓	R	Card sent to him & to McClure Court	4/8
		Yeats-Brown, Maj. J.			/	/	✓		

Kennedy Rev D J (Revd. Donald James Kennedy)
Lane AD (A. D. Lane)
Lane DR (D. R. Lane)
Lazenby JG (J. G. Lazenby)
Miller AJ (A. J. Miller)
Paine AJ (A J. Paine)
Proctor A (A. Proctor)
Robertson AM (A. M. Robertson)
Sykes Victor J (Victor J. Sykes)
Thom Ed F (Ed F. Thom)
Thompson TH (T. H. Thompson)
Walter EH (E. H. Walter)
Thompson Col HS (Col. H. S. Thompson)
Spencer Col Richard (Lt-Col. Richard Augustus Spencer DSO)
Dulling Albert K (Albert K. Dulling)
Green CH (C. H. Green)
Minylees Jas (James Minylees)
Crawford Thos (Thomas Crawford)
Inches RC (R. C. Inches)
Ainslie Tait D (D. Ainslie Tait)
Ball JP (J. P. Ball) -
Shipman (S. C. Eustace Shipman)
Wardlaw Ramsay B (B. Wardlaw-Rainey)
Foster PC (P. C. Foster)
Yeats-Brown Maj J (Maj. J. Francis Yeats-Brown)

3

		S	K	Y	F			
126	Drummond F.B.H	1	1	.				
	Foster P.C.			✓				
	Hood. R			✓				
	Thompson N.A.			✓				
	Lawton Harold			✓				
	May Norman			✓				
	Hogg Ja Emma			✓	19 Upham Park Rd. Chiswick			
	Popham F.H			✓	Bosgrove Vicarage. Chichester	Halnaker	205	
	Dickson H~A (Ec.Rafon Cht)			✓	37E Elgin Cres. H 11			
1	Baker Arthur E. (R)			✓	36 Highfield Av. Kingsbury N.K 9	COL 7563		
	Swain. Francis			✓	36 Harrington Rd	Ken 9054		
	Coost. John. (C/A)			✓				
	Topokoff B.Onis			✓	4 Eardley Crescent S.W.5	FLA 2669		
	Horst John. L			—	32 Grange Rd Chiswick	CHI 4217		
140	Honey Thomas			—	12 Bute St.	KEN 1311		
	Graham Margaret J							

1876

70

Drummond FBH (F. B. H. Drummond)
Foster PC (P. C. Foster)
Wood R (R. Wood)
Thompson NA (N. A. Thompson)
Lawton Lancelot (Launcelot Lawton)
Hay, Norman (Norman Hay)
Hogg Jas Emerson (James Emerson Hogg)
Popham FH (F. H. Popham)
Dickson Wm A (William Dickson)
Baker Wm A (Eec Reform Club) (William A. Baker)
Baker Arthur E. (A) (Arthur E. Baker)
Swain, Francis (Francis Swain)
Coast, John (C/A) (John Coast)
Topokoff B (Brian Toporkoff)
Hirst John L (John L. Hirst)
Hosey Thomas (Thomas Hosey)
Graham, Marquess of (James Angus Graham, Marquess of Graham, later 7th Duke of Montrose)

21

W	LADIES	S	Y	K	Received Badge	£ — S — D	Card	Yearly £ . S . D
	Mrs Ramsay	+		✓		5 5 0		5 5 0
	Hon Mrs Ramsay	+		✓		1 1 0		1 1 0
	Mrs Spencer			✓		10 6		10 6
	Mary Newnham			✓		10 6	R	10 6
	S. Fuller			✓	5		✓	
	Edith Ingrove			✓	1	1	R ✓	
	Mrs Tate	Mrs		✓		10		
	Princess de Chimay			✓	1	22 Sloane Avenue		
	Lady Ronald Graham			✓		2 6	R ✓	
	Lady Brindley				10 6	R ✓	10 6
	Lady Sillman				2 10 0	25 Gloucester Place	
	Maria Endean (Miss)	✗		✓	1 7 6	R ✓	
	Joan Endean "			✓	2 6	R ✓	
	Booth Mrs H.			✓		R ✓	
	Ashford Miss E			✓		Link ✓	
	Ayerst Miss E			✓			
	Beckett Mrs R.			✓		R ✓	
	Blincher Princess			✓		R ✓	
	Bothamley Miss			✓		R	
	Erskine Mrs ?			✓		R ✓	
	Erskine Miss V			✓		R ✓	
	Houghton Mrs E			✓			
	Jacqueson Louetua			✓			
28	Makino Lady			✓	(secretarial)	R ✓	
25	Mellor Mrs N			✓		R ✓	

Ladies

Mrs Ramsay
Hon Mrs Ramsay (Hon. Ismay Lucretia Mary Ramsay)
Mrs Spencer (Maud Evelyn Spencer, née Ramsay)
Mary Newnham (Mary Garneys Newnham, née Latter)
Dr Fuller
Edith Cazenove
Mrs Tate ((Maybird) Mavis Constance Tate, née Hogg)
Princesse de Chimay
Lady Ronald Graham (Lady Ronald Graham (Nancy Edith Graham, née Baker)
Lady Brindley
Lady Saltoun (Dorothy, Lady Saltoun, née Welby)
Marie Endecno (Miss)
Joan Endecno (Miss)
Booth Mrs H (Mrs H. Booth)
Ashford Miss E (Miss E. Ashford)
Ayassot Miss E (Miss E. Ayassot)
Beckett Mrs R (Ruth Beckett)
Blucher Princess (Princess Evelyn Mary Blücher von Wahlstatt, née Stapleton-Bretherton)
Bothamley Miss (Margaret Bothamley)
Erskine Miss R (Miss R. Erskine)
Erskine Miss V (Miss V. Erskine)
Haughton Mrs E (Mrs E Haughton)
Macqueen Constance (Constance Macqueen)
Makins Lady (Lady Makins)
Mellor Lady N (Lady N. Mellor)

			Badge	£	s	d		Cond	£	Yearly s	d
	26	Thomson Mrs L.		✓				C/A			
		Wicken Ethel		✓			expires				
		Williamson Nellie		✓							
June 3rd		Elderton Mrs M		✓				McP			
"	30	Van Leurp. Anne		✓				LA			
.		Foster Mrs EM		✓				McP			
.		Carstairs-Jones Mrs		✓				LA			
		Edmonstone Miss CL		✓				IFL			
		Eckersley Mrs		✓				IFL			
"		Sword Mrs Denston		✓				McP			
		Cameron Mrs M.R.		✓				McP			
		Fuller Mrs EA		✓				Q			
S		Walker Mrs		✓							
		Chatfield Mrs	K	✓					1	1	-
S	40	Clark Mrs Lady		✓							
.		Curtis Eileen		✓				Lmil			
		Dyson Mrs A.		✓				? Lady			
		Dyson Mr J.		✓				? "			
		Egerton (Mrs Joss		✓							
		Friend Mrs D		✓							
		Hedger Miss J.		✓		1	1	.		1	1	.
		Hsuich Mrs KI	Y	✓				Mrs			
		Hoare Mrs J.		✓							
		Kennedy Mrs Bond		✓							
	50	Lindsay Violet		✓							

Thomson Mrs L (Mrs L Thomson)
Wickers Ethel (Ethel Wickers)
Williamson Nellie (Nellie Williamson)
Elderton Mrs M (Dr. Ethel Mary Elderton)
Van Lennep, Anne (Anne Van Lennep)
Foster Mrs EM (Mrs E. M. Foster)
Carstairs-Jones, Mrs (Mrs Carstairs-Jones)
Edmonstone Miss CL (Miss C. L. Edmondson)
Eckersley Mrs (Francis Dorothy Eckersley, née Clark)
Sword, Miss Deniston S (Miss S. Dennistoun Sword)
Cameron Miss EA (Miss E. A. Cameron)
Fuller, Miss EA (Miss E. A. Fuller)
Walker Mrs (Mrs Walker)
Chatfield Mrs (Mrs Chatfield)
Clerk Hon Lady (Hon. Mabel Honor Clerk, née Dutton)
Curtis, Eileen (Eileen Curtis)
Dynon Miss A (Miss Abbie. Dynon)
Dynon Mrs J (Mrs J. Dynon)
Egerton Mrs Foss (Mrs Foss Egerton)
Friend Mrs D (Mrs D. Friend)
Hedges Miss J (Miss J. Hedges)
Hind Miss KI (Miss K. I. Hind)
Hoare Mrs J (Mrs J. Hoare)
Kennedy Mrs Donald (Mrs Donald Kennedy)
Lindsay Violet (Violet Lindsay)

MacQueen Constance (Constance MacQueen)
Patrice Mrs O'C (Mrs. O'C Patrice)
Riddell, Miss Enid (Enid Riddell)
Symonds Miss K (Miss K. Symonds)
Tesch Miss D (Miss D. Tesch)
Volkoff Miss A (Anna Wolkoff)
Fuchs-Vordkoff Frau von (Frau von Fuchs-Vordkoff)
Tolemasn, Miss Irene (Miss Irene Tolemans)
Hillo Miss E (Miss E. Hillo)
Cowan Mrs Alec (Mrs Alec Cowan)
Ken Clark Lady B (Lady B Ken Clark)
Homer Dr A (Dr A. Homer)
Dawberry Pauline (Pauline Dawberry)
Horsefield Mrs (Averil) (Mrs Averil Horsefield)
Bacon Mrs H (Mrs H. Bacon)
Beckett Mrs AB (Mrs A. B. Beckett)
Brown Miss Nancy (Miss Nancy Brown)
Clench Miss June (Miss June Clench)
Cox Miss Hilda (Miss Hilda Cox)
Dell Miss FG (Miss F. G. Dell)
Egan Kathleen (Kathleen Egan)
England Miss Pat (Pat England)
Harvey Mrs Nellie (Nellie Harvey)
Hollier Miss (Miss Hollier)
Jones Mrs E (Mrs E. Jones)

	Macbeth Miss N.			M			
	Miller - Charlotte			M			
	Ramsay Mr Zoe			RF			
	Selby - D' Vincent		/ · /	RF	(Sect Hook)		
80	Sparrow Elizabeth			M			
	Steadman - Doris			BUF			
	Sullivan Miss F			M			
	Sullivan Miss M			M			
	Turner Mrs CA			M			
	de Wendt Mrs E			M			
USA	Dalling Mrs A W			R			
	Lowry Miss Mona			M			
	Hammond Mr M.			R	his		
S	Mr Ogilvie			R			
G 90	Lady Ogilvie			M			
S	Lamb Miss J.B.S.			M			
	Mackinnon Mrs Fred			R	Lib Nat		
	Amor. Marjorie		/ / -	R			
	Lees. Madeline ( )		/ / -	R			
	Randolf Mrs Randy						
	Kurd Mrs						
	Stanford Mrs			R	20 Pi Gate Terrace		KES 6692
	Taylour Mrs Fay						BAY 2909
	Topokoff Mrs						
100	Nicholson Mrs (C)				8 Ashburn Gdn		FRO 0805

Macbeth Miss N (Miss N. Macbeth)
Miller Charlotte (Charlotte Miller)
Ramsey Mrs Zoe (Zoe Ramsay)
Selby Dr Viscountess (Dorothy Evelyn (née Grey), Dowager Viscountess Selby)
Sparrow Elisabeth (Elisabeth Sparrow)
Steadman, Doris (Doris Steadman)
Sullivan, Miss F (Miss F Sullivan)
Sullivan, Miss M (Miss M Sullivan)
Turner Mrs C A (Mrs C. A. Turner)
De Windt Mrs E (Mrs E De Windt)
Dulling Mrs AW (Mrs A. W. Dulling)
Lowry Mrs Mona (Mrs Mona Lowry)
Hammond Mrs M (Mrs M Hammond)
Mrs Ogilvie
Lamb Miss JBS (Miss J. B. S. Lamb)
Mackinnon Mrs Fred (Mrs Fred Mackinnon)
Amor, Marjorie (Marjorie Amor)
Lees Mrs Madileine (Mrs Madeleine Lees)
Yarndell Mrs Maude (Mrs Maude Yarndell)
Wood Mrs (Mrs Wood)
Stanford Miss (Miss Stanford)
Taylor Miss Fay (Miss Frances Helen 'Fay' Taylor)
Topokoff, Miss (Miss Topokoff)
Nicholson Mrs (C) (Mrs Christabel Sybil Nicholson)

Wards			Parish			
Co. Ordinating Ass						
NCU						
Nordic League						
Pink Ascp	Patriot	Free Press	Meetings	Literature		
Spain chumps	Protocol	Financial	Foreign			
N Ratepayers A						
Nat Soc Party						
Nationalists						
Liberty R. League						
10 IFL						
Medical						
City						
Perth						
Edinburgh						
Angus						

180

80

Wards   Panels

Co-Ordinating Ass
NCW
Nordic League
Illegible   Patriot   Free Press   Meetings   Literature
Illegible   Protocol   Financial   Foreign
N Ratepayers A (National Ratepayers Association)
Nat Soc Party (National Socialist Party)
Nationalists
Liberty R League (Liberty Restoration League)
IFL (Imperial Fascist League)
Medical
City

(Editors' note: This page shows the beginnings of an attempt to unify the patriotic societies and sort them by group, locality and specialisation)

Perth
Edinburgh
Angus

Wardens —

S	Lord Carnegie		E. H Cole	
S	Lord Colum Stuart		Dr Mellotte	
	Mr Cross		Wm Joyce	
	The Duke of Wellington			
	John Bailey			
	Peter Agnew			
S	Lord Sempill			
	Sir Alexander Walker			
	Sir James Edmundstone			
S	Lord Galloway			
	Lord Redesdale			
	Alex Cowan Esq			

Wardens

Lord Carnegie (Lord Charles Alexander Carnegie, later 11th Earl of Southesk)

EH Cole (Commander E. H. Cole)

Lord Colum-Stuart (Lord Colum Crichton-Stuart MP)

Dr Mellotte (Dr James Henry Mellotte)

Mr Cross (John Carlton Cross)

Wm Joyce (William Joyce)

The Duke of Wellington (Arthur Charles Wellesley, 5th Duke of Wellington)

John Bailey (John Bailey, later 2nd Baronet)

Peter Agnew (Lt-Commander Sir Peter Garnett Agnew, MP)

Lord Sempill (Col. William Forbes-Sempill, 19th Baron Sempill)

Sir Alexander Walker

Sir James Edmunstone (Sir Albert James Edmondson MP)

Lord Galloway (Randolph Algernon Ronald Stewart, 12th Earl of Galloway)

Lord Redesdale (David Bertram Ogilvy Freeman-Mitford, 2nd Baron Redesdale)

Alex Cowan Esqr (Alec Cowan)

Stewards

S	Harold Mitchell	MP		Edinburgh	Hughes Jones	
S	Thomas Hunter	MP			Crawford C. H...	
S	Sir Samuel Chapman	MP			Sh. J...	
	John Vannek					
	L Featherstone Hamond					
	O.C. Gilbert					
	Sir Ernest Bennett	MP				
	Cuthbert Reavely					
	Richard Findlay		7			
10	J Ruckbrook					
	J Mitchell		7			
S	H Luttman Johnson					
	H Cowper					
	H.T Mills		7			
	Somers Capt					
S	Hughes Jas					
S	Batturck Harry					

Stewards

Harold Mitchell MP (Col. Harold P Mitchell MP)
Thomas Hunter MP (Provost Thomas Hunter MP)
Sir Samuel Chapman MP (Sir Samuel Chapman MP)
John Vanneck (John Vaneck)
C Featherstone Howard (C Featherstone-Hammond)
OC Gilbert (Oliver Conway Gilbert)
Sir Ernest Bennett MP (Sir Ernest Bennett MP)
Cuthbert Reaveley (Cuthbert Reaveley)
Richard Findlay (Richard Fitzgerald Findlay)
G Rushbrook (J. F. Rushbrook) CHECK !!!
J Mitchell (John Mitchell)
H Luttman Johnson (H. T. 'Billy' Luttman-Johnson)
H Cooper
H T Mills (Herbert T. 'Bertie' Mills)
Somers Capt (Captain Somers)
Minylees Jas (James Minylees)
Borthwick Harry (Brig.-Gen. Francis Henry Borthwick DSO CMG)

185

HOUSE OF COMMONS

	Badge			
May—	✗	Peter Agnew	W	
	✓	Sir J. Edmondson	W	
	✓	Harold Mitchell		S
	✓	Mr Tate		S
	✓	Brown K Hunter	.	S
	.	Sir Ernest Bennett		S
	.	Lord Colum Stuart	.	W
	✓	A H M R	.	W
	✓	Sir Samuel Chapman	.	S
10	✓	John McKie		S
	✓	John Stourton (Hon)		S
		Kerr. Col. C.I.		

20

House of Commons

Peter Agnew
(Lt-Commander Sir Peter Garnett Agnew (Conservative; Camborne))
Sir J Edmundson
(Sir Albert James Edmondson MP (Conservative, Unionist; Banbury))
Harold Mitchell
(Col. Harold Paton Mitchell (Conservative, Unionist; Brentford and Chiswick))
Mrs Tate
(Maybird Mavis Tate, née Hogg (Conservative, West Willesden 1931; Frome 1935))
Provost Hunter
(Provost Thomas Hunter (Conservative; Perth and Kinross))
Sir Ernest Bennett
(Labour, Cardiff Central)
Lord Colum-Stuart
(Lord Colum Crichton-Stuart (Conservative, Unionist; Northwich))
A.H.M.R.
(Captain Archibald Henry Maule Ramsay (Conservative, Unionist; Peebles and South Midlothian))
Sir Samuel Chapman
(Sir Samuel Chapman (Conservative, Unionist; South Edinburgh))
John McKie
(Conservative, Galloway)
John Stourton (Hon)
(John Joseph Stourton (Conservative, South Salford))
Kerr. Col. C.I.
(Col. Charles Iain Kerr, later 1st Baron Teviot (Liberal, Montrose Burghs))

Speakers

	France	Spain	Poland	France		Press
Loveday — Arthur		•				
Chesterton, A.K.						•
Findlay, Richard	•					
Yaunck, Jno.	•					
Mills	•					
Collier Cott						
Houston, J.						
Dalrymple A.D.				•	•	

Speakers

                          Finance | Spain | Poland | France | Press

Loveday, Arthur   *
(Arthur Loveday)
Chesterton AK   *
(Arthur Kenneth Chesterton)
Findlay Richard   *
(Richard Findlay)
Vannek John   *
(John Vaneck)
Mills   *
(H. T. V. 'Bertie' Mills)
Collier Alf
(Alfred Collier)
Houston J
(Richard Allistair 'Jock' Houston)
Dalrymple AD (Poland, France)   *   *
(A. D. Dalrymple)

Kriters

Lowday. A.
Peacourt. Prof.
Chesterton. A.K.

Writers

Loveday. A. (Arthur Loveday)
Pencourt. Prof (Professor Pencourt)
Chesterton AK (Arthur Kenneth Chesterton)

70955

F. S.

John Bailey
Dick Spencer
R. Prior

Richard Findley
Ronald Graham
Gillespie
Bromley Trench
David Waddilove
Aubrey Leese
Gillot
Joyce

L.1.

Gillcot
Joyce
W. Darnell
Rutherston
Mitchell
J-Hammond
Autecka
Lease
Joyce
Hunter

L.2.

Yate Brown
Sirrlen
Lockay
Vas
Ludwin
Miles
Lattman-Johnston

FS
John Bailey
Dick Spencer (Lt-Col Richard Spencer)
R Prior
Richard Findlay (Richard Fitzgerald Findlay)
Ronald Graham (Lord Ronald Graham)
Galitzine (Prince Yurka Galitzine)
Brinsley Trench (Brinsley Le Poer Trench)
David Wedderburn (David Scrymgeour-Wedderburn)
Aubrey Lees
Gilbert (O. C. Gilbert)
Joyce (William Joyce)

L.1
Gilbert, deleted (O. C. Gilbert was interned in September 1939)
Joyce, deleted (William Joyce left for Berlin in August 1939)
McDermott (?)
Rushbrooke (J. F. Rushbrook)
Mitchell (John Mitchell)
F-Hammond (C. Featherstone-Hammond)
Chesterton (A. K. Chesterton)
Leese (Arnold Spencer Leese)
Joyce (William Joyce)
Houston (Jock Houston)

L.2.
Yeats-Brown (Francis Yeats-Brown)
Savolea (Charles Sarolea)
Loveday (Arthur Loveday)
Voss (?)
Ludovici (Anthony Ludovici)
Mills (H. T. 'Bertie Mills)
Luttman-Johnston (H. T. W. 'Billy' Luttman-Johnson)

Editors note: the purpose of this page is open to speculation. 'F.S.' may represent an initial attempt to assemble Staff along military lines; L.1 and L.2 may represent a plan to mobilise two regional cells (two 'London' subdivisions?)

> Written the day after
> War was declared on Germany

Land of dope & Jewry
Land that once was free
All the Jew boys praise thee
Whilst they plunder thee
    Poorer still & poorer
    Grow thy true born sons
    Faster still & faster they're
        They're sent to feed the guns

Land of Jewish finance
Fooled by Jewish lies
In press & books & movies
While our birthright dies
    Longer still & longer
    So the rope they get
    But — By the God of Battles
    T'will serve to hang them yet.

Above: Manuscript on House of Commons writing-paper, 'Land of Dope and Jewry' written by Ramsay on the day after War was declared on Germany.

Right: Printed leaflet, Hymn 1939 ('Land of Dope and Jewry')

HYMN 1939

Land of dope and Jewry,
Land that once was free,
All the Jew boys praise thee
While they plunder thee.

    Poorer still and poorer
    Grow the true born sons,
    Faster still and faster
    They're sent to feed the guns.

Land of Jewish finance,
Fooled by Jewish lies,
In press and books and movies
While our birthright dies.

    Longer still and longer
      Is the rope they get
    But, by the God of battles
    T'will serve to hang them yet.

1369/2

J. WELLWOOD JOHNSTON
Chairman
G. I. CLARK HUTCHISON
Hon. Treasurer
Miss MARGT. H. KIDD
Hon. Secretary

TELEPHONE No. 22732

SCOTTISH 1924 CLUB
103 PRINCES STREET
EDINBURGH, 2

2nd June 1939.

Captain A.H. Maule Ramsay, M.P.,
    Kellie Castle,
        ARBROATH.

Dear Captain Ramsay,

        I do hope you will forgive me for not communicating with you sooner. During the past week or two I have been particularly busy and have not been able to devote as much time as I should like to the organising of another meeting.

        Apropos of the formation of a Co-ordinating Committee, I have contacted several people and I must say that some are extremely diffident about being actively associated with such a proposal. Nevertheless, I have stressed the unofficial character of such a Committee and the fact that there should be no publicity attached.

        I have succeeded in getting the co-operation of the following:-

    Mr S.C. Eustace Shipman - Rotary Club.
    Mr James Amos -   Business Club.
    Mr A.V. Todd -   University.
    Mr Robert Bell -   Edinburgh Parliament,
and Captain Crawford. Captain Down of the British Legion I think /

Above: First page of a letter (remainder missing) to Ramsay written on 1924 Club writing-paper

The Right Club A-Z

Agnew, Lt-Cdr Sir Peter Garnett (1900-1990) Education: Repton. Career: Royal Navy; Conservative MP for Camborne Central; ADC to Governor of Jamaica 1927-28; Trustee of The Historic Churches Preservation Trust. Clubs: Carlton, Royal Cornwall Yacht. Views: Peter Agnew was described in his *Daily Telegraph* obituary as 'something of a right-winger, perhaps out of naivety rather than conviction.' Richard Griffiths suggests that his connection with the Right Club 'is likely to have been based on naivety coupled with knee-jerk right-wing reactions'. On May 11 1942 he wrote to *The Times* about railway station vending machines, suggesting 'that the many thousand penny-in-the-slot machines which adorn, or rather assist in disfiguring, almost every railway station in the country should make their first and final contribution to the Government scheme for scrap iron.' See Introduction for his views on the fate of Romanian Jews.

Ainslie Tait, D.

Amor, Marjorie alias of Marjorie Mackie, MI5 agent recruited by Charles Maxwell Knight to infiltrate the Right Club and monitor the activities of Anna Wolkoff and Tyler Kent. She played a key role in their arrest, prosecution and imprisonment.

Applegate, A. J.

Ashford, Miss E.

Ayassot, Miss E.

Bacon, Mrs H.

Bailey, John Milner, later 2nd Baronet Education: Winchester. Background: married in 1932 Diana, eldest daughter of Winston Churchill. She divorced him in 1935 and subsequently married Churchill's political ally, Duncan Sandys. Bailey's father, Sir Abe Bailey, the South African mining magnate, was a good friend of Winston Churchill's. Abe Bailey was notable for the part he played (or nearly played) in the Ramsay Macdonald blackmail affair. The Prime Minister had, in the 1920s, written pornographic letters to a mistress in Vienna. In 1929 the mistress, seeing Macdonald about to embark on his second term as PM, decided that the time had come to cash in. Abe Bailey put up the money to buy back the letters, while J. H. 'Jimmy' Thomas, the Trade Unionist and Labour politician soon to become Lord Privy Seal, was elected 'bagman' and despatched to Paris to settle up. Unfortunately Thomas, in the words of his young assistant Oswald Mosley, 'sidelined to Monte Carlo and lost the lot', leaving the Foreign Office and MI6 to pick up the pieces. The letters were bought and destroyed, no copy having been made, though Sir Charles Mendl of MI6 recalled a line that went something like 'Porcupine through hairy bowers shall climb to paradise'.

Baker, Arthur E. Printer; produced material for the British Union of Fascists; detained under Defence Regulation 18b.

Baker, William A. listed in the Red Book as a member of the Economic Reform Club, a think tank founded by Edward Holloway and others in the 1930s and that was later to become the Economic Research Council (Edward Holloway wrote *Money Matters*, an autobiographical account of his early days with the Economic Reform Club).

Ball, J. P.

Beatty, John

Beckett, Mrs A. B.

Beckett, Ruth Member of the British Union of Fascists; wife of boxer Joe Beckett. They were both detained under Defence Regulation 18b during the war. Joe Beckett enjoyed a parallel career as a film actor, starring as Tom Cribb in Harry B. Parkinson's 1926 film *When Giants Fought*, one of a series of boxing films, *Romances of the Prize-Ring*. The film tells the story of Cribb's fight against Tom Molyneaux, the black slave who became American Heavyweight Champion. (Parkinson, a pioneer of the gripping, information-rich 'short', also made *Tense Moments from Opera* (1926) and *Cosmopolitan London* (1924), an intriguing documentary about minority groups in London, featuring 'Chinamen', 'Negroes' and 'Asiatic-lascars'.)

Bennett, Geoffrey

Bennett, Sir Ernest Nathaniel Education: Durham School and Hertford College, Oxford. Career: served with the Oxford and Bucks Light Infantry in the Boer War and First World War; originally a member of the Liberal Party, he was first elected to the House of Commons in 1906 but defeated in the General Election of 1910; joined the Labour Party and was elected for Cardiff Central in May 1929. Views: Bennett backed the Arab cause in Palestine and was in favour of maintaining good relations with Germany. Whilst he did 'frankly deplore Germany's harsh treatment of her Jewish subjects' he nevertheless felt that Russia, 'whose ceaseless endeavours to ridicule and destroy the Faith of Christ' appeared 'infinitely more odious to thoughtful men and women in this country than any features of Germany's domestic policy.' Background: For a while he pursued a successful career both as an author – his book *The Downfall of the Dervishes* ran to three editions – and an Oxford don. He gained Firsts in Mods and Literarae Humaniores at Oxford and a First in Theology before being elected to a Fellowship of Hertford. He was J. G. Fremantle's tutor and relates how he 'gave a lecture in the Schools on the recent Sudan campaign and, by way of illustration, dressed up Jack Fremantle and two other undergraduates in Dervish jibbahs and spears I had brought back from the Omdurman battlefield. At the end of the lecture the three 'dervishes' led by Jack, broke loose, and ran shouting up the High and along the Corn and Broad, followed by an ever-increasing crowd. The porter of Trinity, who had opened the gate, suddenly caught sight of the wild Dervishes within a few yards, and as he banged the door in alarm Jack Fremantle hurled his spear, which stuck quivering in the woodwork.' He went on to praise his former pupil's fortitude in the face of a terminal illness, saying that Fremantle lived as 'a friend beloved by many, and died without an enemy in the world.'

Blücher von Wahlstatt, Princess Evelyn Mary, *née* **Stapleton-Bretherton** (1876–1960) Background: Princess Blücher von Wahlstatt was born into the Catholic landed gentry, a daughter of Frederick Stapleton-Bretherton of Rainhill Hall, Lancashire. Her husband, the fourth Prince Blücher, was descended from the Blücher who played a key role in the allied victory at Waterloo. Views: Princess Blücher spent the First World War in Germany and wrote an interesting account of her life there, *Princess Blücher, English Wife in Berlin: a private memoir of events, politics and daily life in Germany throughout the War and the social revolution of 1918.* This memoir gives a useful account of the events leading to the German Revolution, describing the disintegration of the German *ancien regime*, the abolition of the monarchy and the advent of the Weimar Republic. The Princess was a member of the Anglo-German Fellowship and the Nordic League.

Booth, Dr. Meyrick a regular contributor to the right-wing publications *The Patriot* and *Truth* and author of several pamphlets including *Peace and Power.* He translated *Rudolf Hess's Peace Mission*, the account by Hess's wife. Views: pro-German, covertly anti-Semite.

Booth, Mrs H. wife of Meyrick Booth.

Borthwick, Brig-Gen. Francis Henry 'Harry' DSO CMG a prominent figure in Ramsay's parliamentary constituency, Peebles and South Midlothian.

Bothamley, Margaret An active member of Nordic League, The Link, the Imperial Fascist League and the British People's Party. The parties in her flat at 67 Cromwell Road, South Kensington, were well-known and frequented by the smart right-wingers such as Lord Ronald Graham and the formidable lesbian policewoman, Commander Mary Allen. She kept a signed photograph of Hitler on her piano, was an occasional speaker at the Ilford and Ealing branch of The Link. She married Lt-Col Charles Strong, a member of the British Union of Fascists.

Brindley, Lady

Brocklehurst, Sir Philip Lee (1887-1975) MI5 agent, recruited by Charles Maxwell Knight to infiltrate the Right Club. Education: Eton and Trinity Hall, Cambridge. Career: served with the Life Guards in the First World War; attached to the Egyptian Army, 1918-20: in World War II commanded the 2nd Regiment of the Arab Legion Desert Mechanized Brigade; later worked with the British Council in Palestine Trans-Jordan. Achievements: he was a member of Ernest Shackleton's Antarctic Expedition of 1907-09 and one of the team led by Sir Edgeworth David in the first ascent of Mount Erebus in 1908.

Brooke, Harold

Brown, Miss Nancy Contributer to the *Anglo-German Review* (see Introduction). Member of the Militant Christian Patriots.

Cameron, Miss E. A.

Cannton, John

Carnegie, Lord Charles Alexander Carnegie, KCVO, later 11th Earl of Southesk (1893-1992) Warden of the Right Club. Education: Eton. Career: Scots Guards, for a while ADC to the Viceroy of India. Private life: in 1923 he married Princess Maud of Fife, granddaughter of Edward VII, his fellow Right Club member and brother Scots Guards officer the Earl of Galloway acting as best man. When questioned by a journalist in 1990 he denied any knowledge of the Right Club, but recalled his near-neighbour Ramsay, describing him as ' a very loyal, patriotic man'. Views: Until he was well into his nineties Carnegie supplied appropriately inflammatory right-wing sound-bites. Some were banal ('The whole trend of violence has escalated because there is no penalty – like the cat and death...'); others were witty, such as his proposed sale of the Falkland Islands to Argentina for £10m payable in ten convenient installments: 'The Argentinian flag could be flown below the Union Jack – starting halfway up the pole and then ascend yearly one tenth of the remainder until it reaches the top'. He was a long-standing member of the Monday Club.

Carstairs-Jones, Mrs

Cazenove, Edith *see* Foreword by Julia Stonor Camoys

Chapman, Sir Samuel MP (1859-1947) Career: Conservative MP for Edinburgh South from 1922 and served on the Conservative Party's Perthshire Education Committee. Views: He campaigned vigorously against the immigration of German Jews to Britain and supported Ramsay's Aliens Restriction (Blasphemy) Bill. Achievements: knighted in the 1920 New Year Honours for 'valuable war work, especially in connection with the Perth and Perthshire Prisoners of War fund [and] Public and local services'.

Chatfield, Mrs

Chesterton, Arthur Kenneth (1896-1973) see Introduction. A. K. Chesterton was prominent in right-wing circles from the 1930s until his death in 1973. From 1934 he was active in Mosley's BUF, edited its magazine, *Action*, and wrote *Portrait of a Leader*, a biography of Mosley. He broke with the BUF in 1938 but remained active on the right-wing scene. Unlike Mosley and a great many others of the Right, he was firmly against appeasement and felt that the only way to create and sustain a truly independent fascist Britain was to defeat Germany – a view that suggests he had a clearer perception of Hitler's global aspirations than did many of his right-wing contemporaries. From the start, the Security Services took a close interest in him, blocking his appointment when he applied for the post of home services editor of the BBC. In 1954 he founded the League of Empire Loyalists, a pressure group campaigning against the dissolution of the British Empire and the progressive granting of independence to former colonies. His most notable achievement was his role in the foundation of the National Front in February 1967. This organization, still active today and therefore in a sense a legacy of the Right Club, was an amalgamation of the Racial Preservation Society, the British National Party and the League of Empire Loyalists. He served with the Durban Light Infantry in World War 1, winning the Military Cross.

Clark, Lady B Ken

Clarke, Richard Member of the Imperial Fascist League.

Clench, Miss June

Clerk, Hon. Mabel Honor, *née* **Dutton** wife of Sir George James Robert Clerk, 9th Baronet, of Penicuik House, Midlothian. The Clerks were prominent figures in Ramsay's constituency.

Coast, John

Cole, Commander E. H. An extreme anti-Semite, member of the Nordic League and Chancellor of the White Knights of Britain. The White Knights of Britain, also known as The Hooded Men, championed among other things the revival of the Statute of Jewry of 1275, swearing an oath of allegiance to Edward I in whose reign it was passed[8]. The Statute imposed tight restrictions on ownership of land by Jews and effectively outlawed Jewish money-lending. Ramsay's last major campaign as a Member of Parliament was to table a motion for its revival.

Collier, Alfred

Collier, Capt. Vincent Collier alias 'Hawke' and 'Captain X', a man of shadowy and complex loyalties. A prominent member of the British Union of Fascists, he later joined Joyce's National Socialist League. As an Irish ex-army officer and former Sinn Fein member, he admired Mosley's support for Irish

---

[8] See Appendix 2, The Statutes of Jewry 1275.

independence and his rigorous criticism of British policy in Ireland. He spied on right-wing organisations for the Jewish Board of Deputies, having been recruited by Harold Laski.

Cooper, H.

Cooper, Mr

Corbett, E. S.

Cork, A. C.

Coverdale-Sharpe, Revd. George Unitarian Minster and member of the Nordic League and The Link. He memorably attacked the Bishop of Durham (Herbert Hensley Henson) for having had 'the audacity to say that our Lord was a Jew'. His resolutely pro-Nazi views were unpopular with the church and caused his son, who later became well known as the novelist Tom Sharpe, much embarrassment when he was a schoolboy.

Cowan, Alec a member of Ramsay's Constituency Committee.

Cowan, Mrs Alec wife of Alec Cowan.

Cox, Miss Hilda

Cox, Thomas

Crawford, Thomas

Crichton-Stuart, Lord Colum Edmund Education: Oxford. Career: Conservative (Unionist) MP for Northwich in Cheshire; with the Foreign Office until 1920; Background: third son of the 3rd Marquess of Bute. He was related to Ramsay by marriage, Ramsay's wife being the widow of his nephew, Lord Ninian Crichton-Stuart. Views: Roman Catholic; deeply preoccupied with the Communist threat to Christianity. He was associated with Lord Glasgow in the Christian Defence Movement.

Cross, John Carlton Secretary of the Co-ordinating Committee of the Right Club, set up to unify existing right-wing groups and societies in Britain.

Curtis, Eileen

Dalrymple, A. D. listed in the Red Book on the 'Writers' page as a specialist on Poland and France.

Daubeny, Pauline see Dennistoun Sword, Lt (John) Colin

de Chimay, Mary Brenda (nee Hamilton) Princesse daughter of Lord Ernest William Hamilton and Pamela Campbell and wife of Lt-Col Prince Alphonse de Chimay of the Scots Guards. The de Chimays lived at 22 Sloane Avenue, Chelsea.

de Munck, Helene a member not listed in the Red Book since her membership post-dates Ramsay's last update of the ledger. A Belgian, she was one of the three female MI5 agents, with Majorie Amor and Joan Miller, sent in to infiltrate the Right Club by Maxwell Knight. De Munck was a clairvoyant and, as such, an ideal *agent provocateur* in the Kent-Wolkoff affair. She won the superstitious Anna Wolkoff's confidence by telling her fortune.

De Windt, Mrs E

Dell, Miss F. G.

Dennistoun Sword, Lt (John) Colin married to the half-sister of Prince Yurka Galitzine, whose name appears next to his in the Red Book, suggesting that they joined at the same time. Education: Harrow. Career: served in France 1939–40 as Captain in the 1st Battalion Gordon Highlanders; wounded and taken prisoner 1940 (a cutting from *The Times* announcing this appears interleaved in Prince Yurka Galitzine's War Diary); Barrister, Lincoln's Inn, 1944; genealogist from 1955. Background: married 13 Sept 1939 (*divorce* 1966) Pauline Vincent, formerly Daubeny, wife of Reginald E. J. Daubeny, and only daughter of the late Henry S. Turner by his wife Emma Lilian Fawcett Hodgson (afterwards Princess Nicholas Galitzine).

Dennistoun Sword, Miss S was a member of the Militant Christian Patriots. She and Lt J. C. D-S were related to W. Dennistoun-Sword, co-author with Henry S. L. Alford of *The Egyptian Soudan: Its Loss and Recovery*.

Devereaux, Alan

Dickson, William A a pro-Nazi interned under Defence Regulation 18b; a member of the Economic Reform Club.

Down Captain J.

Drummond, Captain George Henry Career: Diana Mitford's bank manager; Chairman of Drummond's Bank; High Sheriff of Northamptonshire. Views: a prominent member of The Link and of the British League for the Abolition of Vivisection. The Link had an active local branch in Northampton of which Drummond and the local Labour Councillor Wenman Bassett-Lowke were both members. Northampton was also the scene of some notable anti-Semite outbursts, in particular an incident reported by the *Northampton Independent* when a pig's head, dripping with blood, was hung above the door of the local synagogue. Drummond was on the 18b suspect list and had been found in possession of an illegal high-frequency radio. He is also reported to have cut down a copse of trees for the purpose of spying on a neighbouring airfield. Despite this, he was not formally arrested or interned alongside other 18b suspects. Instead, he announced that he was no longer able to 'fit in' with 'life as it is lived in the average English community', and was therefore moving to the Isle of Man. Since Drummond had influential friends, among them the Prince of Wales and the Chairman of the Bank of England, Montagu Norman, it is not impossible that he used his influence to avoid arrest and internment. His chauffeur, Jack Brooks, recalled him meeting Heydrich and Hitler when abroad. Ribbentrop was a guest at the

Drummond country seat, Pitsford Hall. It is said that he had a swastika, now concealed, emblazoned on the bottom of the Pitsford Hall swimming pool. There are also rumours of fancy-dress parties in the 1930s at which guests arrived in SS uniforms. Pitsford Hall, now the home of Northamptonshire Grammar school, was for a while the home to a Polish Convent School – attended by Rula Lenska.

Drummond, F. B. H. member of the South Africa Branch of the Ancient Order of Froth Blowers of the Royal African Society[9].

Dulling, Albert K.

Dulling, Mrs A. W.

---

[9] In 1933 Drummond attended a Royal African Society dinner in honour of the Duke of Brabant, heir to the Belgian throne. At this dinner, one of the purposes of which was to celebrate Britain's co-operation with Belgium in successful commercial schemes in the Belgian Congo, one of the speakers was the 2nd Viscount Leverhulme. His father, William Lever, 1st Viscount Leverhulme, is well known as the founder of Lever Brothers and the creator of Port Sunlight, a model community near inhabited exclusively by Lever Brothers employees, who enjoyed good facilities and a high standard of living in exchange for a strict and clearly-defined commitment to work. One of the prime ingredients of Lever Brothers soap was palm oil, a commodity cheaper and more plentifully available in the Belgian Congo than it was in Lever's main source of supply, British West Africa. Lever, with Belgian blessing, struck a lucrative deal in which Lever Brothers developed their own plantations in the Belgian Congo on mutually agreeable terms. As was the case with their counterparts in Port Sunlight, the Congolese workers were expected to work very hard – but there the resemblance ended, and British and Belgian archives are replete with protests by missionaries, doctors and administrators about the inhumane treatment of workers on the Lever Brothers estates. These were issues of which few of the many society luminaries who attended the 1933 dinner can have been aware. Their guest speaker, William Lever's son, offered an upbeat picture of Anglo-Belgian endeavours in the colonies and spoke eloquently of Britain's dual commitment to business and philanthropy. "At the time there were many hard-headed business men in West Africa who regarded my father's commitments in the Belgian Congo as a philanthropic undertaking, but its eventual practical success showed that native welfare and commercial soundness are not incompatible ideals."

Dynon, Miss Abbie A debutante who appeared regularly in the Court Circular of *The Times* throughout the late 1930s; a member of the well-known Dynon family of Melbourne, her coming out in London appears to have been supported in part by the Mansel-Pleydell family who gave dances for her; her brother James, formerly at Melbourne University, read Law at Christ Church College, Oxford, and was goalkeeper for the Oxford XI; in February 1939 she attended a lecture given by Hilaire Belloc at Seaford house, Belgrave Square: 'The Nature of English Verse'. This event was in aid of the Society of Our Lady of Good Counsel. Duff Cooper presided.

Dynon, Mrs J. wife of J. F. Dynon and mother of James and Abbie; active socialite; attended a concert at the Austrian Legation in December 1937 in the presence of the Duke and Duchess of Gloucester: the programme featured Sidonie Goossens (harp), Nathan Milstein (violin), Ivor Newton (piano) and The Trapp Choir of Salzburg, who sang old madrigals and Austrian folk songs and played Pandean pipe music. Also present were the Hon. Mrs Borthwick, the Dean of Windsor, Lady Colefax and Dr Crowley.

Eckersley, Francis Dorothy *née* Clark second wife of the distinguished electrical engineer and broadcaster Peter Pendleton Eckersley. Ironically, she too became a broadcaster, in Germany – alongside William Joyce, Margaret Bothamley and John Amery.

Eckersley, Peter Pendleton (1892-1963) an electrical engineer who pursued three interlinked careers, with the BBC, with independent radio and with MI6. He was chief engineer of the BBC until sacked by Lord Reith, a hard-line Scots Calvinist who disapproved of Eckersley's adultery though he was himself an adulterer. Reith's piety consistently overcame his instincts for tolerance, as is witnessed by his disapproval not only of adultery but also of the airing of light entertainment on Sundays. The resulting BBC embargo on Sunday broadcasting opened up all manner of opportunities for entrepreneurs, one being Captain

Leonard Plugge, who with Eckersley's assistance set up the enormously successful IBC (International Broadcasting Company). In 1938 IBC broadcast 'light' programmes from transmitters in Europe and captured as much as 80% of the Sunday audiences. Eckersley also worked for Marconi's Wireless Telegraph Company based near Chelmsford. He sang and read poems on air for 2MT, the first licensed radio station in Britain and an offshoot of Marconi. From 1937 he helped MI6 develop its own home-grown propaganda broadcasts to counteract those from Nazi Germany.

Eddis, Lt-Col Bruce Lindsay DSO

Edmondson, Miss C. L. member of the Imperial Fascist League.

Edmondson, Sir Albert James Conservative MP for Banbury. Education: University College School. Career: served in World War I and was gassed at Passchendale; recovered in 1918 and appointed to the Staff of Eastern Command; He was a member of the Conservative Party and of Oxfordshire County Council (1922-37); elected to the House of Commons in 1922; Parliamentary Secretary to the Ministry of Pensions (1925-31); Assistant Government Whip (1937) Views: He was involved in a campaign to repatriate Basque child refugees who had found refuge in England in the wake of the Spanish Civil War (see Introduction).

Egan, Kathleen

Egerton, Major J.

Egerton, Mrs Foss

Elderton, Dr. Ethel Mary (1878-1954) Member of the Militant Christian Patriots; Assistant Professor at University College, London, where she was a Galton Scholar and held a Fellowship. Views: a statistician who had a strong interest in

Eugenics and Demography; co-authored a number of books with her brother Sir William Palin Egerton.

Endecno, Joan

Endecno, Marie

England, Pat

Erskine, Miss R.

Erskine, Miss V.

Featherstone-Hammond, C Official of the National Citizen's Union; a Steward of the Right Club.

Findlay, Richard Fitzgerald Member of the Council of the Nordic League and Vice-Chairman of the Central London Branch of The Link. Background: A former member of the Royal Flying Corps, he cut a dashing figure. Before he contested the Wavertree By-election, Mosley said of him 'He'll get the women's vote. They like 'em over thirty. With hair on their chest.' Views: Prominent anti-communist; gave an anti-Semite talk in June 39, 'The Hidden Hand of European Affairs', denouncing Jewish 'domination' of high finance.

Fitzpatrick Lewis, Capt. J.

Foster, J. P.

Foster, Mrs E. M. Member of the Militant Christian Patriots.

Foster, P. C.

Friend, Mrs D.

Fuchs-Vordkoff, Frau von

Fuller, Dr

Fuller, E. A.

Fuller, Miss E. A.

Galitzine, Prince (Yuri) 'Yurka' (Nikolaievitch) (1919-2002) see Introduction. Galitzine was born in Yokohama, Japan, the only son of Prince Nikolai Alexandrovitch Galitzine (1899-1963) and Emma Lilian Fawcett-Hodgson. Rita Kramer, in her memoir *Flames in the Field*, recalls Galitzine's role as an intelligence officer in the Political Warfare Department of Supreme Headquarters Allied Expeditionary Forces (SHAEF). In December 1944 he was sent as part of a small team into Natzweiler concentration camp. As a result, he wrote a report on his findings (see Introduction). After the war, Galitzine was a prominent campaigner for peace and improved communications in international relations. He was a pioneer of what was then a comparatively new phenomenon, the Public Relations agency. His own PR company, Galitzine & Co, represented Conservative Party interests in Africa, principally in the Federation of Rhodesia and Nyasaland. Yuri Galitzine died on 28 November 2002 and is buried at Clipsham Church.

Galloway, Randolph Algernon Ronald Stewart, 12th Earl (1892–1978); son of Randolph Stewart, 11th Earl; member of the Anglo-German Fellowship; President of Galloway Constituency Conservative Association. Background: brother officer of Lord Carnegie's in the Scots Guards and best man at Carnegie's wedding to Princess Maud of Fife. He was a high-ranking Freemason; a brother Mason said of him that 'Lord Galloway applied a twinkling severity to his Freemasonry. His perfect knowledge of ritual and his natural kindliness of nature married well, and as a former officer in the Scots Guards things had to be right.'

Gilbert, Oliver Conway founder member of the Nordic League and a keynote speaker of the BUF. In 1938 he was closely associated with a suspected Japanese spy and may also have been a target for recruitment by the Abwehr. He was detained in September 1939 under 18b and released in February 1944. He resumed his involvement in extreme right-wing activities after the war.

Graham, F. J. G.

Graham, James Angus Graham, Marquess of Graham, later 7th Duke of Montrose elder brother of Lord Ronald Graham; served as a Lieutenant Commander in the RNVR; belonged to several anti-Semite organizations in the 1930s; settled in Rhodesia after the World War II and became a staunch 'white supremacist', serving in Ian Smith's rebel Rhodesian Front government as Minister of Agriculture Lands and Natural Resources (1962-65); Minister of Agriculture (1964-65); Minister of External Affairs and Defence (1966-68). Views: Montrose favoured the 'hang-em-and-flog-em' approach characteristic of Lord Carnegie (*q.v.*) and others, once warning in a typically fervid speech that 'the Beatles, international finance groups, colonial freedom movements and student agitators were all agents of a communist plot to achieve world domination'. As a result of his involvement with the Smith regime, Montrose was banned from the House of Lords, a state of affairs that triggered some debate about parliamentary procedure and human rights.

Graham, Lady Ronald (Nancy Edith Graham, *née* Baker) wife of Lord Ronald Graham

Graham, Lord Ronald Malise Hamilton Graham (1912-1978) second son of the 6th Duke of Montrose brother of the Marquess of Graham (*q.v.*). Education: Stowe. Career: Royal Navy. Views: an active and prominent member of The Right Club and many other right-wing organizations including The Link.

Graham, R.

Green, C. H.

Hammond, Mrs M

Harvey, Nellie

Haughton, Mrs E

Hay, Norman Education: Imperial College; Career: built up the BSA subsidiary, Monochrome, an electro-plating concern. His own electro-plating company, Norman Hay, floated in 1972 offering 1.4m shares at 48p. The business owned a six-acre site adjacent to Heathrow. Views: involved with Launcelot Lawton in the right-wing International Policy group; a protégé of Lord Northcliffe's.

Hedges, Miss J.

Hillo, Miss E.

Hind, Miss K. I.

Hirst, John L.

Hiscox, Gertude Blount 'Mollie' Though not recorded in the Red Book she was, as the mistress of Jock Houston (*q.v.*) sufficiently actively involved in the Right Club to be considered a *de facto* member. Background: Founder member of The Link; helped Leigh Vaughan Henry set up the National Citizen's Auxiliary Service; she and Norah Briscoe, a typist in the Ministry of Supply, were arrested and charged with passing information to a Harald Kurtz who, though they supposed him to be a German agent, was in reality an MI5 plant: they were sentenced to five years imprisonment. Views: openly pro-Hitler (see Introduction);.

Hoare, Mrs J.

Hogg, James Emerson Hogg sheltered Jock Houston and Mollie Hiscox when they were on the run in 1940; lived at 19 Upham Park Road, Chiswick.

Hollier, Miss

Hollyce, L. J.

Holmes, A.

Homer, Dr A. Dr. Occasional contributor to *The Catholic Herald*. He wrote in 1933 that 'The Soviet movement was Jewish, not a Russian conception. It was forced on Russia from without...'

Horsefield, John

Horsefield, Mrs Averil

Hosey, Thomas

Houston, (Richard Allistair) 'Jock' East End painter and decorator, convicted criminal, the rough diamond of the Right, his 'cockney presentation with a crude political anti-Semitism [...] drew a positive response from many in his audience' (Thurlow, *Fascism in Britain*). In the predominantly middle-class and aristocratic milieu of the Nordic League and The Link, his was the voice of a 'man of the people'.

Hughes, Captain James McGuirk A soldier of fortune in the regiment of idealists; alias 'P. G. Taylor' and 'Mr Cunningham'; ran 'Department Z', Mosley's intelligence and propaganda unit; ran a private anti-left-wing intelligence agency partly funded by Cunard, to whom he supplied blacklists of potential Union agitators; retained by Scotland Yard via Special Branch to keep an eye on Union activities; burgled to order the head offices of the International of Labour Unions in 1924; on 9 April 1940 Lord Ronald Graham introduced him to Anna Wolkoff, to whom he handed an envelope addressed to Herr W. B. Joyce, Rundfunkhaus, Berlin containing 'some good anti-Jewish stuff'; Hughes also worked, under the alias Cunningham, for MI2, a department of the Security Services focusing on Germany's intentions in Scandinavia.

Hunter, Provost Thomas MP Education: Perth Academy. Career: journalist; member of the Conservative Party; County Councillor for Perth 1919-32; Chairman of the Perthshire Education Committee; 1935 elected MP for Perth; Lord Provost of the Royal Burgh of Perth. Views: leading campaigner against the immigration of German Jews into Britain.

Inches, R. C.

Jones, Mrs E.

Jones, N

Joyce, William (1906-1946) an American national of Irish extraction who obtained British nationality by deception, also known as 'Tom Long' and, 'Lord Haw-Haw'. Joyce was a senior member of Oswald Mosley's British Union of Fascists before he left and founded the National Socialist League in 1937. He studied at Birkbeck College for while and gained a reputation as a speaker. He fled to Germany in August 1939 and throughout the Second World War broadcast anti-British propaganda, becoming known as 'Lord Haw-Haw', a sobriquet he owed to 'Jonah Barrington', the pseudonymous radio critic of the *Daily Express*. It was descriptive of his sarcastic, sinister, hectoring tone, the broadcasts always beginning with the particularly memorable catch-phrase '*Jair*many calling! *Jair*many Calling!' Initially he had been unable to find work in Berlin, and he owed the job at the Runfunkhaus to fellow Right Club member Dorothy Eckersley, herself an exile and a popular broadcaster of propaganda. It is held that 'Barrington' might easily have been describing any of the well-known broadcasters – Norman Baillie Stuart, Eduard Dietze, Joyce or Wolf Mitler; but it is to Joyce that name irrevocably stuck. In appearance he was a short, compact man with a livid scar across his face and piercing eyes. The journalist Cecil Roberts described a typical Joyce speech: 'Thin, pale, intense, he had not been speaking for many minutes before we were electrified by this man... so terrifying in its dynamic force, so vituperative, so vitriolic'. The reaction of the British public to the Lord Haw-Haw broadcasts was mixed. A poll commissioned by the BBC suggested that after initial alarm at some of his pronouncements, he came to be regarded as a welcome sideshow offering humorous diversion from the rigours and banalities of war. There was a popular song entitled 'Lord Haw-Haw the Humbug of Hamburg', the 'hee-hawing, high-browing Hun', performed by the Western Brothers, a popular duo of the time who specialized in sending up the upper classes. Joyce was finally arrested at Flensburg, on the run near the German-Denmark border. His voice gave him away. Captain Alexander Lickorish and Lieutenant Perry, two British officers who encountered him while they were looking for firewood, immediately recognized it. Joyce had not been able to resist helping them in their search for fuel, speaking in English as he did so. Back in Britain, he was tried on three counts of Treason but convicted on only one. The doubtful question of his true nationality formed the basis of his defence, but the Attorney General, Sir Hartley Shawcross, successfully argued that since Joyce possessed a British passport, albeit illegally obtained, he owed allegiance to the Crown. After an unsuccessful appeal he was hanged in January 1946 – the executioner was Albert Pierrepoint – and remained unrepentant to the end. 'In death as in life, I defy the Jews who caused this last war, and I defy the power of darkness they represent.'

Kennedy, Mrs Donald wife of the Rector of Cottesbrooke.

Kennedy, Revd Donald James Education: Jesus College, Cambridge. Career: Rector of Cottesbrooke, Northampton. Views: Unrecorded, but probably not openly at variance with those of the patron of Cottesbrooke, Captain The Hon. Reginald Narcissus Macdonald-Buchanan MC of Cottesbrooke Hall: Scots Guards, Master of the Pytchley Hounds, Director of Distillers' and member of the Guards', the Turf and Buck's. For a brief account of right-wing activities in Northampton, see *Drummond, Captain George Henry*.

Lamb, Miss J. B. S.

Lane, A. D.

Lane, D. R.

Lawrence, Walter B.

Lawton, Launcelot involved with Norman Hay in the Information and Policy group and its magazine, *Information and Policy*; a protégé of Lord Northcliffe's.

Lazenby, J. G.

Le Poer Trench, William Francis Brinsley, later 8th Earl of Clancarty Education: Pangbourne. Undistinguished as a right-wing activist he achieved some standing as a leading 'Ufologist', firmly committed to a belief that the earth might at any moment be overcome by an alien invasion. In the early Thirties Brinsley Trench, as he was known, is reported in the Court Circular as having given away his sister Lady Alma Le Poer Trench in marriage and having attended high-profile society events such as the King's Levee. He then goes off radar until the Fifties when he began to air and publish his views on extra-terrestrial life: Trench believed not only in flying saucers but also in the Hollow Earth theory. The seven titles he inherited in the peerages of Britain, Ireland and the Netherlands were nothing to him since he could, he claimed, trace his descent from 63,000 BC, when alien beings had first landed on Earth. He claimed that most of us were descended from these immigrants: 'This accounts for all the different colour skins we've got here.' Not all of the aliens had come from space. Some migrated from an underground civilisation that 'still existed beneath the Earth's crust.' They had emerged from tunnels at a number of places including the polar ice caps and Tibet. 'I haven't been down there myself,' Trench said, 'but from what I gather [these beings] are very advanced.' Publications: *The Sky People*, 1960; *Men Among Mankind*, 1962; *Forgotten Heritage*, 1964; *The Flying Saucer Story*, 1966; *Operation Earth*, 1969; *The Eternal Subject*, 1973. *Secret of the Ages*, 1974 He was editor of *Flying Saucer Review*. He founded of the International Unidentified Object Observer Corps and a House of Lords UFO Study Group.

Lee, G. W.

Lees, Aubrey Career: colonial civil servant; Deputy-Governor of the Jaffa District in Palestine until recalled in 1938 as a result of overtly anti-Semite and pro-Arab activities. Views: member of the Nordic League and The Link; fiercely anti-Zionist, he supplied details of alleged Jewish atrocities in Palestine to right-wing groups in London.

Lees, Mrs Madeleine

Leese, Arnold Spencer (1878-1956) see Introduction. A fanatical anti-Semite, he expressed pro-Nazi views (though he moderated these after the German invasion of Norway). Leese had founded the Imperial Fascist League in 1928. He was imprisoned for 6 months in 1936 for libelling Jews in the *The Fascist*. When named on a detention order issued under the Defence Regulations after the outbreak of the World War II, he went into hiding, but was eventually arrested in November 1940.

Lentayne, B.

Lindsay, Violet

Longhurst, M. B.

Loveday, Arthur Listed in the Red Book as an author, he wrote a pro-Franco account of the Spanish Civil War, *World War in Spain* (1939).

Lowry, Mrs Mona

Ludovici, Anthony Mario (1882-1971) see Introduction. Career: secretary to Rodin; artist; philosopher and social critic. Views: hard-line anti-Semite; proposed that society should be run on aristocratic principles and that inter-breeding between races should be avoided, since it led to the depletion of vigorous native stock; a champion of Eugenics; believed in preventing the diseased and (his word) 'botched' from reproducing, if necessary by surgical intervention.

Luttman-Johnson, H. T. W. 'Billy' Secretary and founder member of the January Club, an offshoot of the BUF, he also founded the right-wing Windsor Club which attracted members such as Henry Fairfax-Lucy and Douglas Jerrold. He was active in Friends of National Spain along with Colonel Rupert Dawson of Braco. He was a friend of Francis Yeats-Brown, C. G. Grey (see correspondence between C.G.G and L-J in Introduction), J. F. C. Fuller, George Lane-Fox Pitt-Rivers and Major Davidson-Houston. He founded Forgan's Debating Club, a society that was as socially glittering as it was hard-line right-wing. Views: interned under 18b for his pro-German stance; the following letter, written to a female friend in Germany, was read out in court: 'I am not the only person in Britain who, thank God, loves Germany and the Germans. [ ] It is we, not the warmongers, who are patriots. [ ] Some people seem to think that if we do not win, the Germans will become all-powerful. My answer is: Let Germany be all powerful. Germany rules well and wisely and will keep good law and order. [ ] There is room in the world for Germany and Britain. Let the Germans have the Continent and let us keep our own sea possessions.' His application for *habeas corpus* was unsuccessful, his case not helped by the disclosure in court of a letter he had sent to William Joyce, congratulating him on the Lord Haw-Haw broadcasts.

Macbeth, Miss N.

Mackinnon, Mrs Fred

Macqueen, Constance

Makins, Lady

McDermott

McKie, John Hamilton Education: Harrow and Christ Church, Oxford. Career: Conservative MP for Galloway, 1931. Clubs: Bachelors'; Pratt's; New, Edinburgh. Views: preoccupied with the Soviet 'threat' and to a lesser extent the Judaeo-Bolshevik plot theory; in favour of restoring Germany's colonies;

saw the march into Rhineland as 'a revolt against what the German people thought was a wrong oppression'; pro-Hitler on the question of the alleged persecution of Lutheran churches.

Mellor, Lady N.

Mellotte, Dr James Henry Little was known about Mellotte until documents were released describing MI5's deepening concern, in 1942, that the Irish Republic might serve as springboard from which to launch a Nazi invasion. The Security Services ran a covert military exercise, Victor 2, a war-game scenario examining the feasibility of such an invasion. Whilst the exercise was hypothetical, there were real 'suspects', a number of Irishmen in Birmingham and London who had been under surveillance as a result of their supposed Nazi sympathies. Mellotte, an occupational ophthalmologist at the Royal Eye Hospital in London, was one of them. He was known to be a friend of Ramsay's and was said to have been dining at Claridges with him one evening when Ramsay had said 'These bloody Yids, I hate the bastards! I had lunch yesterday at the German Embassy with Ribbentrop!' Views: not recorded; Ramsay thought sufficiently highly of Mellotte to appoint him a Warden of the Right Club; Ramsay might have wished to embark on an Irish recruitment drive in much the same spirit as he had drummed up support in Scotland: Mellotte, a respectable professional based in London, might well have proved useful in such an enterprise.

Miller, A. J.

Miller, Charlotte

Miller, Joan MI5 agent; an infiltrator of the Right Club. Born in 1918, she joined MI5 shortly before the war after a spell at Elizabeth Arden. She worked under Lord Cottenham[10], head of

---

[10] **Pepys, Sir Mark Everard (6th Earl of Cottenham)** 'Cotty' to his friends and mistresses. An amateur racing driver, the Earl was an early pioneer of road safety and made a number of broadcasts on this subject in the 1920s. He

the transport section, then for B5b, the political subversion unit, where Maxwell Knight set her to spy on the Right Club. She and fellow-agent Marjorie Amor testified at the Tyler Kent trial, confirming that secret documents had been passed by Anna Wolkoff to the Duca del Monte, the Assistant Naval Attaché at the Italian Embassy. Miller was Maxwell Knight's mistress for while but the arrangement did not last, Miller tiring of being used as a front to mask Knight's homosexuality. She left him and married Tom Kinlock Jones in 1943. She was transferred to the Political Intelligence Department (PID). Her memoir, *One Girl's War: Personal Exploits in MI5's Most Secret Station*, was published in Ireland in 1986 despite some opposition from MI5.

Mills, Herbert T. V. 'Bertie' Chairman of the Central London Branch of the Link; member of the Imperial Fascist League, the Nordic League and Lord Lymington's British Council against European Commitments; contributed to *New Pioneer*; prominent in the People's Campaign against War and Usury; a strong supporter of National Socialism; a member of the Nordic League and Right Club and an associate of leading British fascists. He was detained under Defence Regulation 18b between May 1940 and June 1943.

Minylees, James

Mitchell, Col. Sir Harold Paton MP Education: Eton, Sandhurst, University College, Oxford. Career: (1900-1983) Conservative MP for Brentford and Chiswick from 1931 to 1945; Created 1st Baronet Mitchell of Tulliallan in 1945; Vice-Chairman of the Conservative Party under Winston Churchill. Business interests: Director of the London and North-Eastern Railway Company; the New Zealand and Australian Land Company Ltd; the Ben Line Steamers; Alloa Glass Works Company; Stirling Brickworks (chairman); the New Main Brick

---

was influential in the foundation and development of the Police Driving School at Hendon.

Works Ltd; Alloa Coal Company. In 1920 he rescued the failing Mountain Park Coal Company in Canada which later became a key part of the Mitchell concern, Luscar. He invested in the Globe and Phoenix Gold Mining Company Ltd in Southern Africa. He bought Tulliallan Castle from from the estate of Sir James Sivewright in 1923 and sold it to the Scottish Home Department in 1950 for £9,100. He invested money in a game farm and afforestation projects on the estate. Pastimes: an accomplished downhill skier; set up a pipe band competition in Alloa in the early Thirties; Joint Master of the Lauderdale Hunt; member of The Royal Company of Archers. War service: Liaison Officer with the Polish Army; with Command Welfare Office for the Anti-Aircraft Command. He left the Britain after the nationalisation of a sizeable chunk of his business interests in 1947, taking much of his money with him. He owned extensive properties in the Caribbean and became an authoritative lecture on Caribbean subjects. Clubs: Carlton; Bath; Alpine; New, Edinburgh. Views: pro-Franco; advocated the return of Basque child refugees to Spain (see Introduction).

Mitchell, John member of the United Ratepayers Advisory Committee.

Munro, E

Newnham, Mary Garneys *née* **Latter**

Nicholson, Mrs Christabel Sybil Wife of Admiral Wilmot Nicholson, a signatory of the 1938 Link letter to *The Times*; associated with Anna Wolkoff and Tyler Kent; arrested in possession of a copy of a secret paper obtained illegally from the American Embassy by Kent; tried for offences under the Official Secrets Act and interned but subsequently found not guilty and released. Views: pro-Nazi and took part in the activities of the Right Club.

Norris, John

O' Higgins

Ogilvie, Mrs

Paine, A. J.

Patrice, Mrs. O'C

Pencourt, Professor

Popham, F. H. lived at Boxgrove Vicarage, Chichester; presumably therefore related to Rev Arthur Edgar Popham MC, Vicar of Boxgrove, of the same address.

Pownall, George

Prior, R.

Proctor, A member of the Nordic League

Ramsay, Alec Maule Ramsay's son; outstanding war service with the Scots Guards in World War II; died young of pneumonia in South Africa while Ramsay was interned in Brixton; described in *The Times* as 'a fine forthright character, absolutely fearless and completely full-blooded in all that he did', 'his massive frame, his booming laugh, his gigantic appetite, all bespoke his wholesome geniality and the power of his personality'.

Ramsay, Captain Archibald Henry Maule 'Jock' (1894-1955) MP and wartime detainee, founder of the Right Club, married the Hon. Ismay Lucretia Crichton-Stuart (*q.v.*). Education: Eton, Sandhurst. Career: with the Coldstream Guards in France; severely wounded in 1916; invalided out in 1919 after attachment to the War Office; elected Conservative (Unionist) MP for Peebles and South Midlothian in 1931; parliamentary representative to the Potato Marketing Board, 1936; interned under Defence Regulation 18b during World War II; resumed his seat immediately upon his release in 1944 but was deselected in the general election of 1945; in 1952 wrote *The Nameless War*, an unqualified apologia outlining the history of Jewish influence down the ages and what he perceived as his own unjust treatment at the hands of the British authorities. Ramsay's activities in parliament became increasingly inflammatory as time went on. In 1938 the International Federation of Freethinkers planned to hold a summit in London. Ramsay and his followers denounced this as a 'Godless Conference' and Ramsay managed to introduce a Private Member's Bill, the 'Aliens Restriction (Blasphemy) Bill' which would have prevented the Freethinker delegates from entering Britain. In December he introduced another Private Member's Bill called the 'Companies Act (1929) Amendment Bill' which would require shares in news agencies and newspapers to be held openly and not through nominees. In his speech promoting the Bill, Ramsay claimed the press was being manipulated and controlled by 'international financiers' in New York who wanted to 'thrust this country into a war'. Ramsay was given permission to introduce his Bill by 151 to 104. In December 1938, *The Fascist* (journal of the Imperial Fascist League) declared that Ramsay had 'become Jew-wise' (in other words alive to the idea of a Jewish conspiracy). His only significant action in the remainder of the Parliament was a motion calling for the reinstatement of the Statutes of Jewry passed under King Edward I, a draconian law that severely restricted ownership of land by Jews and had severely cracked down on usury (see Appendix 2). Views: see Introduction.

Ramsay, George Maule Ramsay's son

Ramsay, Hon. Ismay Lucretia Mary (1882-1975) married to Archibald Maule Ramsay, widow of Lord Ninian Crichton-Stuart and daughter of Jenico William Joseph Preston, 14th Viscount Gormanston. Although actively involved in Right Club activities, she was never interned. In January 1939 Mrs. Ramsay gave a speech to the Arbroath Business Club at which she claimed the national press was 'largely under Jewish control', that 'an international group of Jews .. were behind world revolution in every single country' and that Hitler 'must .. have had his reasons for what he did'. The Chief Rabbi for Scotland, Dr. Salis Daiches, wrote to *The Scotsman* challenging Mrs Ramsay. This caused Ramsay severe embarrassment in his constituency, that he nevertheless managed to weather.

Ramsay, Robert Maule Ramsay's son. Views: shared his father's anti-Semitism and believed in the Judaeo-Bolshevik plot theory, writing of his mother's remarks at Arbroath in 1939 'The vain attempts of Rabbi Daiches and Mr Louis Golding to disprove the fact that a group of Jews is behind the world revolution will have convinced no-one'.

Ramsay, Zoe

Randall, Mrs Maud interned under Defence Regulation 18b.

Reaveley, Cuthbert former member of the British Union of Fascists; author of the Foreword to Barry Domvile's 1936 book *By and Large*.

Redesdale, David Bertram Ogilvy Freeman-Mitford, 2nd Baron Fought in the Boer War and the First World War; moved to Canada where he purchased the Swastika Gold Mine; bought the Swinbrook estate in Northumberland and married Sydney 'Muv' Bowles; they had four daughters, Diana Mitford (married Mosley, friend of Hitler's), Jessica Mitford (married Esmond Romilly, left-wing), Nancy Mitford (U and Non-U; *Love in a Cold Climate*) and Unity Mitford (shot herself in Munich, recovered; friend of Hitler's and knew Himmler, Goering and Goebbels). Clubs: Marlborough. Views: felt that Hitler was a 'right-thinking man of irreproachable sincerity and honesty'; member of the Anglo-German Fellowship and The Link.

Riddell, Enid Mary (1903-1973) British racing driver detained under Defence regulation 18b from 1940 to 1943; associated with Anna Wolkoff and Tyler Kent; member of the Nordic League; after the war she moved to Malaga where she owned and ran a club called 'La Rascasse'; smuggled whisky, and was mentioned for it in April Ashley's autobiography.

Roberts, E. A.

Robertson, A. M.

Rowe, T. W. Victor member of the White Knights of Britain; with the British Union of Fascists until 1936; Nordic League; Right Club; Her and O. C. Gilbert were the first Right Club members to be interned under Defence Regulation 18b.

Rushbrook, J. F. Editor of *The Free Press*, organ of the Militant Christian Patriots.

Saltoun, Dorothy, Lady Saltoun, *née* **Welby**

Sarolea, Professor Charles Louis-Camille (1870–1953) see Introduction. Belgian political writer and scholar of French literature; professor of literature at Edinburgh University; founder/owner of Everyman and pioneer of the Nelson Edition, a French language offshoot of Everyman that reprinted the great French classics (in Scotland) and sold them throughout Europe; regular contributor to the *Anglo-German Review*. Views: ingenious pro-Nazi articles and utterances, from offbeat ideas such as the supposed roots of Nazism in Scotland (Carlyle, Houston Stewart Chamberlain) to persuasive exegeses on the German-ness of Danzig.

Scrymgeour-Wedderburn, Lt-Col David, DSO (1912-1944) Education: Winchester and Sandhurst; Career: Lt-Col 1st Battalion Scots Guards; killed at Anzio on 1 March 1944. Background: son of Lt-Col. Henry Scrymgeour-Wedderburn of Wedderburn and Birkhill and Edith Moffat; married Patricia Katherine Montagu Douglas Scott, daughter of Lt-Col Lord Herbert Andrew Montagu Douglas Scott and Marie Josephine Edwards.

Seelig, W. K.

Selby, Dorothy Evelyn (*née* Grey), Dowager Visountess Selby

Sempill, Col William Francis Forbes-Sempill, 19th Baron Master of Sempill; aeronautical engineer; served in First

World War in the Royal Flying Corps, the Royal Naval Air Service and the fledgling RAF; 1920-23 headed a civilian mission to Japan to train Japanese aviators; advised on the formation of the Imperial Japanese naval Air Service, 1921; advised on the reorganization of the Greek Naval Air Service, 1925; believed to have passed sensitive military and technical information to the Japanese; awarded Special Medal of the Imperial Aero Society, Japan; awarded 3rd Order of the Rising Sun. Clubs: Athenaeum, Beefsteak, Junior United Service, MCC. Views: a leading pro-German who argued tirelessly in the House of Lords in favour of peace with Hitler; member of The Link, the Anglo-German Fellowship and the Constitutional Reform Association.

Serocold Skeels, Professor Cecil member of the Nordic League, the United Empire Fascist Party, White Knights of Britain, the Imperial Fascist League; contributor to *Der Sturmer* and other Nazi magazines under his own and assumed names; reported by the Security Services to be seen regularly engaged in research at the British Museum for 'anti-Semitic purposes'; convicted at the Central Criminal Court on 17 February 1941 of offences under the Defence Regulations Act and sentenced to two years' imprisonment; subsequently detained under Defence Regulation 18B.

Shipman, S. C. Eustace member of the Rotary Club, Edinburgh; referred to in the letter interleaved in the Red Book and dated 2 June 1939 from the Scottish 1924 Club, 103 Princes Street, Edinburgh.

Somers, Captain

Sparrow, Elisabeth

Spencer, Lt-Col Richard Augustus 'Dick' DSO Ramsay's brother-in-law. Education: Wellington, RMA Woolwich. Career: served with Royal Field Artillery, 1909; Royal Horse Artillery, 1915; with RFA in France, 1916-19, mentioned twice in Despatches and DSO. Clubs: Army and Navy.

Spencer, Maud Evelyn, *née* **Ramsay** Ramsay's sister, married to Dick Spencer.

Stanford, Mary Agnes Geraldine lived at 20 Queen's Gate Terrace, South Kensington; pro-Nazi; interned under Defence Regulation 18b in 1940.

Steadman, Doris

Stokes, R

Stourton, Hon. John Joseph, MP JP Background: younger brother of the 25th Lord Mowbray. Career: member of the North Russian Relief Force supporting the White Russian Army in Archangel, 1919; elected Conservative MP for South Salford, 1931. Views: made several speeches attacking Jewish immigration and praising the achievements of Hitler in Nazi Germany; anti-Bolshevik; member of the Anglo-German Fellowship; preoccupied with what he saw as the difficulty the authorities might have keeping tabs on Jewish immigrants who had changed or anglicized their names for the purpose (possibly) of fraud, tax evasion, etc.

Sullivan, Miss F

Sullivan, Miss M

Swain, Francis

Sykes, Victor J.

Symonds, Miss Kathleen

Tate, Mavis Constance, *née* **Hogg,** *other married name* **Gott** (1893–1947) politician and feminist. Career: Conservative MP for West Willesden (1931), then Frome (1935); best remembered for her persistent campaign, with Edith Summerskill, for equal pay for women; Chairman of the Equal Pay Campaign Committee, formed in 1943. Views: Mavis Tate dramatically renounced her pro-German views after a nervous breakdown in 1940. After World War II she visited Buchenwald concentration camp to report on the atrocities there, narrating a newsreel of the visit for Pathé News.

Taylor, Frances Helen 'Fay' Career: Irish racing driver and motorcyclist known as 'Flying Fay of Dublin' and 'Miss Fay Taylour, the internationally acclaimed Queen of the Speedways'; won the Leinster Trophy road race in 1934; moved to the United States after the war and worked for a car dealer. Background: educated at the exclusive Alexandra College in Dublin; interned under Defence Regulation 18b as a result of her openly-expressed support for Oswald Mosley and other right-wing figures.

Temple, J

Tesch, Miss D. stenographer

Teviot, Colonel Charles Iain Kerr, 1st Baron DSO MC Career: Lt-Col Royal Horse Guards; mining engineer; senior partner, Kerr, Ware & Co, Stockbrokers; Liberal Party, elected member for Montrose Burghs, 1929; Liberal National MP for Montrose 1932-40; created Baron Teviot, 1930; Chief Whip of the National Liberal Party,1937; Junior Lord of the Treasury 1937-39; Comptroller of HM's Household 1939-40; Chairman of Liberal National Party 1940-56; Chief Whip of Liberal National Party in House of Lords 1945. Views: extreme anti-Semite and subscriber to the Judaeo-Bolshevik plot theory.

Thom, Ed F. member of The Link; distributed the *Free Press*, the anti-Semite organ of the Militant Christian Patriots.

Thomason, Mrs L

Thompson, Col H. S.

Thompson, N. A.

Thompson, T. H.

Tod, A. K.

Tolemans, Irene

Toporkoff, Boris listed in the Post Office Directory as living at 4 Eardley Crescent, London SW5.

Toporkoff, Miss presumably related to Boris Toporkoff.

Turner, Mrs C. A.

Van Lennep, Anne associated with Admiral Barry Domvile, head of The Link, whom she entertained at her flat in Paradise Walk.

Vaneck, John A prominent member of the Nordic League.

Voss

Walker, Alan

Walker, Mrs

Walker, Sir Alexander (1869-1950) Career: whisky magnate; younger grandson of John 'Johnnie' Walker; he and his brother, George Paterson Walker, took the control of the company after the death of their father Alexander Walker in 1889. Views: member of the Anglo-German Fellowship; right-winger; the most generous contributor to the Right Club, making a donation of £100.

Walter, E. H.

Wardlaw-Ramsay, B.

Wellington, Arthur Charles Wellesley, 5th Duke of Education: Eton and Trinity Hall, Cambridge. Career: Grenadier Guards, South Africa 1900. Views: a member of several right-wing groups in the 1930s including the Anglo-German Fellowship; Chairman of the Patriotic Societies; President, Liberty Restoration League; Warden, the Right Club.

Wickers, Ethel

Williamson, Nellie

Wingate, George

Wolkoff, Anna naturalised British subject of White Russian extraction; owned and ran the Russian Tea Rooms in South Kensington with her father, Admiral Nikolai Wolkoff, former naval attaché to the Imperial Russian Embassy in London in 1916. Views: violently anti-Semite and staunchly pro-Nazi, visited Germany on several occasions in the 1930s where she met Hans Frank and Rudolf Hess. Background: met Tyler Kent, an American Embassy cipher clerk, in 1940; introduced Kent to the Right Club and to Archibald Ramsay; Wolkoff, Kent and Ramsay got on and agreed that they shared political views; Kent feared that Roosevelt intended to bring America into the war against Germany: he showed Wolkoff and Ramsay copies of telegrams between Roosevelt and Winston Churchill that supported this view, including some that gave assurances that America would support France in the event of a Nazi invasion. Wolkoff copied these documents and passed them on to the Assistant Naval Attaché at the Italian Embassy, the Duca del Monte. Joan Miller (*q.v.*) and Marjorie Amor (*q.v.*), infiltrating the Right Club for MI5, were party to these arrangements. Soon MI8, the wireless interception service, picked up radio exchanges between Rome and Berlin to the effect that Admiral Wilhelm Canaris, head of the Abwher (German military intelligence), had copies of the Roosevelt-Churchill correspondence. Wolkoff had meanwhile abandoned caution and asked Joan Miller to pass a coded letter to William Joyce (Lord Haw-Haw) in Germany via her Italian contacts. This letter contained comments on Joyce's broadcasts to date and suggestions for the content of future broadcasts on Radio Hamburg. Miller showed the letter to Maxwell Knight, head of B5b, MI5's political subversion unit; on 18 May 1940, Knight alerted Guy Liddell to the Right Club spy ring and its activities. Liddell had an urgent meeting with Joseph Kennedy, the American Ambassador in London. As soon as Kennedy had agreed to waive Kent's diplomatic immunity, Special Branch raided his flat on 20 May, seizing copies of 1,929 classified documents including the Roosevelt-Churchill telegrams.

They also found the Red Book. Wolkoff and Kent were arrested and charged under the Official Secrets Act and tried in secret on 7 November 1940, Wolkoff receiving ten years, Kent seven.

Wood, Mrs

Wood, R.

Yeats-Brown, Major J Francis, DFC Journalist, author and soldier; see Introduction. Education: Harrow and Sandhurst. Career: Kings Royal Rifle Corps, India 1906; 17th Cavalry, Indian Army, India 1907; 5th Lancers, France; Royal Flying Corps, Mesopotamia 1913, Despatches twice and DFC; prisoner in Turkey, November 1915; escaped 1918; retired from Army 1925; editor of *The Spectator* 1926-28; editor of *Everyman*; author of *Lives of a Bengal Lancer* 1930, *Golden Horn* 1932, *Dogs of War!* 1934, *Lancer at Large* 1936, *Yoga Explained* 1937, *The European Jungle*. Clubs: Bath. Views: pro-Franco; pro-Germany; mild, carefully-qualified anti-Semitism; pro-Hitler, believing that Hitler had cured unemployment in Nazi Germany and had created a prosperous society.

Appendix 1

REASONS FOR ORDER MADE UNDER DEFENCE REGULATION 18B IN THE CASE OF CAPTAIN ARCHIBALD MAULE RAMSAY, M.P.

Home Office
Advisory Committee
(Defence Regulation 18B)
London, W.1.

Telephone: REGent 4784
Ref.: . . . R4. . .

24th June, 1940

The Order under Defence Regulation 18B was made against Captain Archibald Maule Ramsay, M.P. Because the Secretary of State had **reasonable cause to believe** that the said Captain Archibald Maule RAMSAY, M.P. had been recently concerned in acts prejudicial to the public safety or the defence of the Realm, or in the preparation or instigation of such acts, and that by reason thereof it was necessary to exercise control over him.

PARTICULARS

The said Captain Archibald Maule RAMSAY, M.P.

Particular (i) In or about the month of May 1939, formed an Organisation under the name of the "Right Club", which ostensibly directed its activities against Jews, Freemasons and Communists. This Organisation, in reality, was designed secretly to spread subversive and defeatist views among the civil population of Great Britain, to obstruct the war effort of great Britain, and thus to endanger public safety and the defence of the Realm.

Reply
The formation of the Right Club, as the attached memorandum shows, was the logical outcome of many years of work against Bolshevism,

carried on both inside and outside the House of Commons, and well-known to all my political colleagues since 1931.

The main object of the Right Club was to oppose and expose the activities of Organized Jewry, in the light of the evidence which came into my possession in 1938, some of which is given in the memorandum.

Our first objective was to clear the Conservative Party of Jewish influence, and the character of our membership and meetings were strictly in keeping with this objective. There were no other and secret purposes.

Our hope was to avert war, which we considered to be mainly the work of Jewish intrigue centred in New York. Later, I and may others hoped to turn the "phoney" war into, not total war, but an honourable negotiated peace.

It is difficult to imagine a body of persons less capable of being "subversive" as this Particular suggests, and coupling this charge with the charge of being 'defeatist" places this whole Particular in the realm of the ludicrous. .

Particular (ii) In furtherance of the real objects of the Organisation, the said RAMSAY allowed the names of the members of the Organisation to be known only to himself, and took great precautions to see that the register of members did not leave his possession or control; and stated that he had taken steps to mislead the Police and the Intelligence Branch of the War Office as to the real activities of the Organisation. These steps were taken to prevent the real purposes of the Organisation being known.

Reply
The real objects of the Right Club being the declared objects, and there being no other objects whatever, the latter part of this Particular is pure fabrication.

There was only one respect in which our aims differed from the Police and M.I., namely, the Jewish question.

Neither Police nor M.I. recognised the Jewish menace. Neither had any machinery for dealing with it, or for withholding information from Jewish members of their personnel.

If names of members of the Club had been placed at the disposal of either of these departments, they would have been seized upon by the Jewish members therein, and reported on to the very quarters from which many members wished them to be withheld.

Particular (iii) Frequently expressed sympathy with the policy and aims of the German Government; and at times expressed his desire to co-operate with the German government in the conquest and subsequent government of Great Britain.

Reply
The latter half of this Particular is a fabrication so preposterous that I propose to treat it with the contempt it deserves.

Lord Marley embroidered this fiction in the Lords a few days after my arrest, insinuating that I had undertaken to be Gauleiter of Scotland under a German occupation of Great Britain.

My solicitors at once invited him to repeat his remarks outside. Needless to say, he did not do so, for there is not a shred of justification for either this Particular or his slanders.

The term "sympathy with the policy and aims of the German Government" is misleading to the verge of dishonesty. It suggests some general agreement or understanding.

Nothing of the kind existed.

I have never been to Germany, and beyond one formal luncheon at their Embassy knew no Germans. What little I had learned about the Nazi system did not appeal to me.

I have never approved of the idea of movements on distantly similar lines being formed in Britain. On the contrary, I disapproved

My view was that the Unionist Party, once enlightened, was the body best suited to take the needful counter-measures to the Jewish plan, and that to do so successfully it did not even need to go outside the powers latent in our Constitution.

In a general way my views concerning German aspirations coincided exactly with those expressed by Lord Lothian in his speech at Chatham House on 29th June, 1937, when he said:

"Now if the principle of self-determination were applied on behalf of Germany in the way in which it was applied against her, it would mean the re-entry of Austria into Germany, the union of the Sudeten-Deutch, Danzig and possibly Memel with Germany, and certain adjustments with Poland in Silesia and the Corridor."

The only aspect of the Nazi policy which contacted in any special way with my views was the opposition to the disruptive activities of Organized Jewry. No patriot -- British, French, German or of any other nationality -- is justified in abandoning the defence of his country to that onslaught, once he has recognized its reality.

To confuse sympathy on this one and loyal point with sympathy with the whole Nazi policy and aims is dishonest; to develop this fallacy into a charge of preferring that system to our own, and being prepared to force that system (of which I disapproved) upon my own country, is the last word in infamy.

Particular (iv) After the formation of the Organisation, made efforts, on behalf of the Organisation, to introduce members of the Organisation into the Foreign Office, the Censorship, the Intelligence Branch of the War Office, and Government departments, in order to further the real objects of the Organisation as set out in (i) hereof.

Reply
Again we have here the fabrication of the wholly unjustifiable charge of a secret and disloyal purpose, already dealt with in Particular (i), and my Memorandum.

In regard to the matter of members of the Right Club and Government offices, I would say this:

The objects of the Club being to spread as rapidly as possible the truth concerning the Jewish danger, time was always a vital factor. From the outset we were in a race with the Jewish propagandists.

To counter them in as many different spheres as possible was obviously the quickest method. Ten members in ten different spheres would spread our information more widely, more quickly than ten members all in the same office or club.

Every political group must follow these lines; this method is the common practice of all political parties.

I never at any time made any effort to get any member a job in any Government Office.

If a member had a choice of two jobs, and didn't mind which he or she took, and asked me about it, I should clearly have replied that as far as the Club was concerned, the sphere in which we had no member to preach the gospel was the one to choose.

For the knowledge to reach such places as the foreign Office, War Office, etc., was obviously to achieve the enlightenment of influential persons most rapidly of all.

Particular (v) After the outbreak of war, associated with and made use of persons known to him to be active in opposition to the interests of Great Britain. Among such persons were one, Anna Wolkoff, and one, Tyler Kent, a Coding Officer employed at the Embassy of the United States of America. With knowledge of the activities in which Wolkoff and Kent were engaged, he continued to associate with them and to make use of their activities on behalf of the "Right Club" and of himself. In particular, with knowledge that Kent had abstracted important documents, the property of the Embassy of the United States of America, he visited Kent's flat at 47, Gloucester Place, where many of the said documents were kept, and inspected them for his own purposes. He further deposited with the said Kent the secret register of the members of the "Right Club", of which Organisation Kent had become an important member, in order to try and keep the nature of the Organisation secret.

Reply

I have never at any time of my life associated with persons whom I have known to be in oppositions to the interests of Britain. On the contrary, my whole record proves that I have devoted more time and trouble than most people to fighting just such persons.

I certainly did not know, and do not now know, that either Mr. Kent or Miss Wolkoff were engaged in activities calculated or likely to harm the interests of Britain.

From my own acquaintance with them both, and conversations I have had during that period, I know they both recognized the activities of Organized Jewry to be one of the most evil forces in politics in general, and one of the most dangerous to the interests of Britain in particular.
All their actions will have been directed to countering those Powers and their designs, and most certainly not to anything that might injure the interests of Britain.

As for myself, I should like to add here most emphatically, in view of various mendacious allegations on the subject that have since reached my ears, that I have never, and of course could never contemplate communicating information to enemy quarters.

Having reasonable cause to believe that the Jewish International intrigues to bring about total war radiated from New York, and knowing that activities were being carried on to sabotage Mr. Chamberlain's policy of pacification and to bring about his over-throw, it was my obvious duty as a Member of Parliament, and one still loyal to Mr. Chamberlain, to make any investigation I could.

I deposited the Red Book of names of the Right Club members at Mr. Kent's flat for the period of my absence from London only after I heard of several persons who had had their papers (dealing with the same sort of subjects as mine) ransacked by persons unknown in their absence.

As I have stated already, I had given explicit assurance of privacy to some of the persons whose names were entered therein. Had their names even come into the hands of the British Secret Police, personated as this force is by Jews, their attitude vis-a-vis the Jewish menace would have become known at once in the very quarters from which they made a particular point of their being withheld, namely, Jewish quarters.

Political burglary is no new thing in this country, when one is suspected of possessing information relating to the activities of Organized Jewry.

Lord Craigmyle, when Lord of Appeal, had his whole house ransacked, every drawer broken open and every paper searched without anything being stolen, at a time when it was reasonable to suppose that his papers contained such matter.

The Chief Lieutenant of Police in Edinburgh declared at the time that it was a "political burglary"; the perpetrators were never traced.

Particular (vi) Permitted and authorised his wife to act on his behalf in associating with, and making use of, persons known to him to be active in opposing the interests of Great Britain. Among these persons were Anna Wolkoff, Tyler Kent, and Mrs. Christabel Nicholson.

Reply
There is no truth whatever in this Particular; and I propose to treat it with the contempt it deserves. Needless to say, the Home Office Advisory Committee produced no evidence to support any of the slanders contained in any of the above Particulars

CONCLUSION
I submit this statement, and the comments on the Particulars, not for my own sake, but to enlighten the country.

When things reach a stage wherein a Lord of Appeal, whose papers are suspected of relating to the plan of Organized Jewry, can be "politically burgled";

When a white Paper containing vital passages on Jewish World-Bolshevism can be immediately withdrawn, and reprinted omitting the vital passages;

When a leading British Industrialist can be blackmailed by Organized Jewry, and coerced into submission by boycott, strikes, acts of sabotage and arson;

When a Member of Parliament, who dares to try and warn the country against this menace of Organized Jewry and their help-mates (the only Fifth Column that really exists in this country) is thereupon imprisoned for three years on false charges;

When these things can happen in Britain, then there must surely be something wrong somewhere.

At a time when Britain and the Empire are engaged in a life-and-death struggle, surely there can be no room for the foul teachings and activities which I have touched upon.

While our sailors, soldiers and airmen are winning victories over the external enemies, surely it is the duty of every patriot to fight this internal enemy at home.

The Prime Minister, in his speech at the Mansion House, stated that he had not become the King's First Minister in order to preside over the liquidation of the British Empire.

There are more ways than one of encompassing the liquidation of the British Empire today; and the National Leder who is determined to counter them all will not only need the utmost support of all patriots, but I believe it will be proved that his most formidable difficulties will emanate from just those very powers which I and other members of the Right Club have all along striven to oppose and expose.

Appendix 2

The Statutes of Jewry

Les Estatutz de la Jeuerie 1275, from The Statutes of The Realm, Vol. 1, page 221.

Usury forbidden to the Jews
Forasmuch as the King hath seen that divers evils and the disinheriting of good men of his land have happened by the usuries which the Jews have made in time past, and that divers sins have followed thereupon albeit that he and his ancestors have received much benefit from the Jewish people in all times past, nevertheless, for the honour of God and the common benefit of the people the King hath ordained and established, that from henceforth no Jew shall lend anything at usury either upon land, or upon rent or upon other thing. And that no usuries shall run in time coming from the feast of St. Edward last past. Notwithstanding the covenants before made shall be observed, saving that the usuries shall cease. But all those who owe debts to Jews upon pledge of moveables shall acquit them between this and Easter; if not they shall be forfeited. And if any Jew shall lend at usury contrary to this Ordinance, the King will not lend his aid, neither by himself or his officers for the recovering of his loan; but will punish him at his discretion for the offence and will do justice to the Christian that he may obtain his pledges again.

Distress for Jews.
And that the distress for debts due unto the Jews from henceforth shall not be so grievous but that the moiety of lands and chattels of the Christians shall remain for their maintenance: and that no distress shall be made for a Jewry debt upon the heir of the debtor named in the Jew's deed, nor upon any other person holding the land that was the debtor's before that the debt be put in suit and allowed in court.

Valuing lands taken for a Jew's debt.
And if the sheriff or other bailiff by the King's command hath to give Saisin (possession) to a Jew be it one or more, for their debt, the chattels shall be valued by the oaths of good men and be delivered to the Jew or

Jews or to their proxy to the amount of the debt; and if the chattels be not sufficient, the lands shalt be extended by the same oath before the delivery of Saisin to the Jew or Jews to each in his due proportion, so that it may be certainly known that the debt is quit, and the Christian may have his land again; saying always to the Christian the moiety of his land and chattels for the maintenance as aforesaid, and the chief mansion.

Warranty to Jews.
And if any moveable hereafter be found in possession of a Jew, and any man shall sue him the Jew shall be allowed his warranty if he may have it; and if not let him answer therefore so that he be not therein otherwise privileged than a Christian.

Abode of Jews.
And that all Jews shall dwell in the King's own cities and boroughs where the chests of the chirographs of Jews are wont to be.

Their badge.
And that each Jew after he shall be seven years old, shall wear a badge on his outer garment that is to say in the form of two tables joined of yellow felt of the length of six inches and of the breadth of three inches.

Their tax.
And that each one, after he shall be twelve years old pay three pence yearly at Easter of tax to the King whose bond-man he is; and this shall hold place as well for a woman as for a man.

Conveyance of land, etc., by Jews.
And that no Jew shall have the power to infeoff (take possession of) another whether Jew or Christian of houses, rents, or tenements, that he now hath, nor to alien in any other manner, nor to make acquittance to any Christian of his debt without the special license of the King, until the King shall have otherwise ordained therein.

Privileges of the Jews.
And forasmuch as it is the will and sufferance of Holy Church that they may live and be preserved, the King taketh them under his protection,

and granteth them his peace; and willeth that they be safely preserved and defended by his sheriffs and other bailiffs and by his liege men, and commandeth that none shall do them harm or damage or wrong in their bodies or in their goods, moveable or immovable, and they shall neither plead nor be impleaded in any court nor be challenged or troubled in any court except in the court of the King whose bondmen they are; and that none shall owe obedience, or service or rent except to the King or his bailiffs in his name unless it be for their dwelling which they now hold by paying rent; saving the right of Holy church.

Intercourse between Jews and Christians.
And the King granteth unto them that they may gain their living by lawful merchandise and their labour, and they they may have intercourse with Christians in order to carry on lawful trade by selling and buying. But that no Christian for this cause or any other shall dwell among them. And the King willeth that they shall not by reason of their merchandise be put to lot and soot nor in taxes with the men of the cities and boroughs where they abide; for that they are taxable to the King as his bondmen and to none other but the King.

Holding houses and farms, etc.
Moreover the King granteth unto them that they may buy houses and castilages in the cities and boroughs where they abide, so that they hold them in chief of the King; saving unto the lords of the fee their services due and accustomed. And that they may take and buy farms or land for the term of ten years or less without taking homages or fealties or such sort of obedience from Christians and without having advowsons of churches, and that they may be able to gain their living in the world, if they have not the means of trading or cannot labour; and this licence to take land to farm shall endure to them for fifteen years from this time forward.

Appendix 3

An extract from the Wiener Library Bulletin (1962 Vol. XVI No.1 page 17) publishing a Despatch from the German Ambassador to the German Foreign Office, Berlin. The Despatch attempts to summarise anti-Semite feeling in Britain immediately prior to World War II.

British Antisemitism was Hitler's Hope

London Envoy's Revealing Despatch of 1939

This despatch by Herr von Dirksen, then German Ambassador in London, which to the best of our knowledge has not been published before, bears the crucial importance which Nazi imperialism attached to the activities of anti-Semites everywhere. A characteristic commentary on the situation sketched in the adjoining column, it may well have reinforced Hitler's determination to launch his war, assured of assistance from Stalin in the East and from the anti-Semite satellites in the West.

Copy 83-26, 19/7 London, 19th July, 1939
German Embassy A.2917
Re: The growth of anti-Semitism in Britain

If the Marquis of Dufferin and Ava, speaking in the House of Lords on behalf of the Government (July 5 last), not only warns against the growth of anti-Semitism in Britain but even stresses that anti-Semitist feelings have always been a vital and inherent factor in the British nation, this is a fact worth noting. It shows that an appreciation of the Jewish question is also on the increase in Britain. Having regard to the stolid, tolerant racial character of the British, every anti-Semitic impulse must be valued all the more highly, since opportunities for disseminating anti-Jewish ideas are very limited. This fact is already reflected by the suppression of all reports of Mosley's Fascist meetings, which are sometimes very well attended, as well as of the anti-Semitism clashes that occur almost daily in East London.

It may be said that Murchin's book, "Britain's Jewish Problem," probably gives the best picture of the present state and development of English anti-Semitism. The book, very conservative and moderate in style, has attracted widespread attention. Right-wing periodicals sometimes open their columns to anti-Jewish contributions.

Even in Conservative dailies, one may read reports - still, for the time being, couched in veiled, indirect language - of Jewish terrorism in Palestine, as well as communiques about anti-British riots among American Jews, incidents which were connected with Jewish boycott threats against British goods (as a protest against British policy in Palestine, which is not sufficiently pro-Jewish). The agitation incited by American Jews is sometimes revealed in a far more menacing light, from the British point of view, than the danger emanating from National Socialist organisations. The Right-wing weekly *New Pioneer* (July, 1939) contains an extremely lively and penetrating article, entitled "Listen, Tommy!" by the well-known writer, Yeats-Brown ("Royal Lancer"). He puts the case for the Palestine Arabs, and criticises British press reports for keeping quiet about certain harsh anti-Arab measures on the part of British troops, while sensationalising anti-Jewish measures in Germany which are, actually, less drastic. The article closes with the unequivocal demand: "Not another British life for Judah."

Anti-Semitic opinions - more or less oblique - also find outlet in a section of the English Catholic press, though only insofar as they reveal Jewish connections with Bolshevism, which is violently attacked in Catholic newspapers.

Apart from the Mosleyites, the Jews are, of course, attacked by individual political, more or less anti-Semitic organizations, in which the very well-connected Conservative Member of Parliament, Capt. A. Ramsay, is beginning to play a definite role.

Another organisation, with Lady Alexandra Hardinge as president, is showing an anti-Semitic film in which, among other things, Jewish ritual slaughter is depicted.

Anti-Semitic attitudes are revealed more clearly by conversations with the man in the street than by press sources. Here, except in Leftish circles, one can speak of a widespread resentment against Jews which, in some instances, has already assumed the form of hate.

The view that the Jews want to drive Britain into war with Germany finds widespread belief. An influential peer maintained recently, for instance, that Britain is threatened with two offensives, German and Jewish. A Right-wing official in the British Diplomatic Service even expressed the opinion recently that the growing British recognition of the Jewish peril would lead to a new orientation of Britain's policy towards Germany.

The alarming increase of Jewish immigration promotes anti-Semitism. The man in the street has the most exaggerated ideas about Jewish immigration - it is believed, for instance, that 30,000 Jews settle in Britain every month, whereas so far only 40-50,000 have come to the United Kingdom. It is often argued that every Jewish immigrant robs an Englishman of a well-paid position. Further, the Englishman cannot ignore the fact that in the confectionery, furniture and catering trades the Jew reigns supreme and advances surprisingly quickly in other fields, the taxi business for instance. Credence is given to the popular rumour that every Jew obtains a weekly family allowance of 9s for each child, whereas the English workman has to manage on 3s a week per child. People notice that Britain's rich Jews have a high standard of living, but leave it to the British people to feed the Jewish immigrants of to collect 6m Marks for the Baldwin Fund, while the ragged British unemployed spend the night on park benches.

Popular feeling is being roused by clever anti-Jewish posters e.g., "Is the British army up to the mark? Yes, sir! Why? It is led by a Jew, fed by a Jew, clad by a Jew." The posters do not fail to mention the names of the Jewish army suppliers.

The growing consciousness of the Jewish question has not served as a warning to philo-Semitic circles. When Jews themselves actually plead, as a excuse for Jewish immigration, that these immigrants, in the event of war, could take over jobs of Englishman going off to the front, that could hardly give comfort to potential front-line soldiers. It must sound insane to German ears, when the suggestion is put forward that the Jews should not be settled collectively, but systematically "infiltrated" into all parts of the country, and all sections of the economy, so that their great talents may be put to better use. However, it could be that the renunciation of the settlement idea, which has been a point to discussion in the House of Commons, originated in complete inability of Jews to cope with agricultural labour in an experimental British work camp.

That many Parliamentarians are still unaware of growing anti-Semitic trends, is revealed by the reproaches hurled at the Government in the House of Commons for their too strict handling of Jewish immigration regulations, and by the requests, submitted there openly almost every day, for privileged landing permits for individual German Jews whose names are specifically given.

It goes without saying that anti-Semitic circles adopt a more or less positive attitude towards the new Germany, and an increase of anti-Semitism goes hand in hand with a growing appreciation of our cause. It should be remembered, however, that anti-Jewish incidents or particular significance, such as occurred last November, are not fully understood, even in anti-Semitic circles, and the efforts of these circles as well as understanding for Germany suffer a setback as a result.

While an increase in anti-Semitism, particularly among the masses, becomes manifest, philo-Semitic circles, all those symptoms notwithstanding, take no adequate counter-measures. A further increase of anti-Jewish feeling in Britain can be expected.

(signed) Dirksen. To the Auswaertiges Amt, Berlin.

Selected Bibliography and Sources

Christie, Agatha: *N or M?*

Dorril, Stephen: Blackshirt: *Sir Oswald Mosley and British Fascism*

Fahey, Father Denis: *The Rulers of Russia*

Griffiths, Richard: *Fellow Travellers of the Right: British Enthusiasts for Nazi Germany 1933-39*

Griffiths, Richard: *Patriotism Perverted, Captain Ramsay, The Right Club and British Anti-Semitism 1939-40*

Jones, Nigel: *Mosley*

Lane, Lt-Col A. H.: *The Alien Menace: A Statement of the Case*

Leese, Arnold: *Out of Step: Events in the Two Lives of an Anti-Jewish Camel Doctor*

Lewis, Wyndham: *Hitler*

Ludovici, Anthony M: (as 'Cobbett') *Jews, and the Jews in Britain*

Ludovici, Anthony M: *A Defence of Aristocracy; A Text Book for Tories*

Ludovici, Anthony M: *The Quest of Human Quality: How to Rear Leaders*

Miller, Joan: *One Girl's War: Personal Exploits in MI5's Most Secret Station*

Mosley, Sir Oswald: *My Life*

Muggeridge, Malcolm: *Chronicles of Wasted Time, Volume Two: The Infernal Grove*

Portsmouth, Gerald Vernon Wallop, 9th Earl of: *A Knot of Roots: an Autobiography*

Ramsay, Captain A. H. M.: *The Nameless War*

Strobl, Gerwin: *The Germanic Isle*

Thurlow, Richard: *Fascism in Britain: A History, 1918-1985*

West, Rebecca: *The Meaning of Treason*

Yeats-Brown, Francis: *European Jungle*

The papers of Capt. H. T. W. Luttman-Johnson (Imperial War Museum)

The papers of Prince Yurka Galitzine (Imperial War Museum)

Anglo-German Review

Country Life

Wiener Library Bulletin

Transcript: Central Criminal Court No. 334, Rex v Tyler Gatewood Kent

Acknowledgements

Thanks are due to friends, colleagues and staff at the London Library, the British Library, the Imperial War Museum and the Wiener Library.